Life at
12 College
Road

Life at
12 College
Road

Eric Mondschein

SOMETHING
OR **OTHER**
PUBLISHING

Edited by Michael Schindler

ISBN 13: 978-0-9846938-3-2

Library of Congress Control Number: 2013954145

Printed in the United States of America
First Printing: 2013
17 16 15 14 13   5 4 3 2 1

Cover design by Rachel Abou-Zeid
Interior design by James Monroe Design, LLC.

SOMETHING OR **OTHER**
PUBLISHING

Info@SOOPLLC.com

For bulk orders e-mail: Orders@SOOPLLC.com
Also available as an e-book.

This book is dedicated to my parents,
Nancy Lee and Morton, and to my brothers,
Jeffrey Mark and Jonathan Thad.

Throughout the writing of this book I have felt especially
close to each of them. And if I listen carefully,
I can almost hear them saying:
"Rick, we don't remember it happening
exactly that way."

CONTENTS

PREFACE

Most of us have never considered that we might be important. And truth be told, by typical standards, we aren't. Only a handful of us ever get to be presidents or generals, or invent or cure something, or become saints for that matter. But that doesn't mean we aren't important to someone.

That's what binds us. We are unquestionably unique, and yet surprisingly similar. And our everyday lives are more important than we may know.

We all have memories—those that make us smile or laugh, others that bring anger or tears, and some that we'd just rather forget. Those memories help to make us who we are today—and in some ways, who we will become tomorrow.

While reflecting upon my past to write this book, I found that it was not the major earth-shattering events that were truly significant for me. Rather, it was the small things, many long forgotten until recently, that deeply touched me. Sure, some of the memories ahead involve fire trucks, police cars, and hospital visits. Not to mention infernos, floods, ice, and a bit of hand-to-hand combat and armed warfare. But most do not. And if their retelling can help you to connect with similar moments from your own life, well, that is special—and well worth the time in my writing these vignettes and your reading them.

So, get yourself a cup of coffee or tea, sit back, and get comfortable. And for a brief period of time, join me for a journey down memory lane, where laughter mingles with tears, sorrow turns to joy, and loss almost becomes bearable.

SILENT WARRIORS

My silent warriors are no more,
Their grandeur given to some strange hiding place
Where only the dust of battles fought in years past
Appears on their unstained uniforms.
Their cannons no longer roar
With the sounds that sent men sprawling,
Nor fill the air with the fruits
Of their harvest.
Their gallant charges are only flickering memories
With the sound of the bugle
And the fall of each man;
As they rushed the mighty fortress
Of the living room chair.

ESM

THE DINING ROOM TABLE

As I sat at the table, I realized the other three chairs had been tilted forward so that their ladder-backs rested against it. They were obviously no longer of use. Scanning the room, it dawned on me that this was not some unknown, foreign establishment—it was the dining room where I shared Sunday dinners with my family for so many years.

I could see my dad sitting at one end of the table, my brother across from me, and my mom at the other end, closest to the kitchen and the telephone. And there was our collie, lying down by my feet. I always thought she liked me best, but that was probably because, somehow, more of my dinner reached the floor than anyone else's.

I remember those meals, with the rich smell of roasts and homemade pies wafting through the house, the banter back and forth, and the laughter. Not that we didn't have rough times—oh yes, there were plenty of those. But there was always laughter.

At every dinner, Dad would hold court. He was a lawyer—a New York City lawyer—and my brother and I would be grilled and cross-examined as to the day's events. He was gruff, but now I know that he was really interested in what we were doing, and wanted to ensure we did it all to the best of our abilities. And may heaven help us if we didn't know what a word meant, or if we used one incorrectly. There was no discussion and no appeals process. We dropped our forks, went to look it up, and came back telling everyone at the table the definition and how to use it in a sentence. I still recall catching the knowing wink or nod between my parents as I got out of my chair and headed for the living room and that dictionary, which took at least two people to carry.

We would often have intriguing company at the table. Some were Dad's clients who had become friends over the years, from local storeowners to international shipping magnates. Others, Mom had gotten to know through her work with the school district or through her faith. These guests were not just from other towns and states, but from all over the world. Although they all spoke English, many had wonderful accents: Jamaican, Persian, Greek, English, Swedish, Kenyan, Ugandan, South African, Australian. They would sit around the table for hours talking, and their laughter would resonate throughout the house. I wish now that I hadn't asked to be excused so soon after finishing one of my mom's pies.

Even when it was just the four of us, that table was lively. Both of my parents were voracious readers, and Mom in particular was a master storyteller. As an avid Agatha Christie fan, she would often bring Miss Marple or Hercule Poirot to life as my younger brother, Jeff, and I hung on every word. Once, shortly after Dad had shared his outrage over the injustice of a black man being seriously beaten for no other reason than being black, Mom began telling us about the book *To Kill a Mockingbird.* We were hooked as she regaled us with the story and its lively characters. We may have been young, but the connection between the book and what Dad had said was not lost on us.

Jeff would usually content himself with eating and making eye contact with me to share his feelings about the conversations swirling around the table. He was more of an observer than a participant, but he would always respond enthusiastically when asked a question. I think he preferred to listen and learn, rather than risk being sent to the dictionary. However, if the conversation dealt with the New York Knicks, Yankees, or Giants, he'd happily hold court.

As I sat alone at the old table, I heard a very unpleasant sound ring out from a distance. The more I listened, the louder it got. At first, the noise seemed not of this world, but eventually, recognition dawned.

My alarm clock—which must have been designed by a sadist.

I threw my legs over the side of the bed and stretched: the start of yet another day. As I rubbed the sleepiness out of my eyes, I recalled the dining room from my dream and those three empty chairs. And it was then that I remembered what had been bothering me for so long: I was alone. You see, my mom, dad, and younger brother have all passed on without me. They are exploring new worlds and I have been left behind. Heck, even my dog is gone.

As I shuffled dejectedly to the kitchen to start the coffee, it hit me: by definition, I am an orphan. I know this to be true, because I still use the dictionary from my parents' living room. It currently resides in our study, patiently waiting to divulge hidden truths to my grandchildren as it did for my brother and me. In fact, the little ones have already discovered it—and its ever-present magnifying glass companion—but they don't yet have any idea what lies within its pages.

2

THE ORANGE CASSEROLE POT

My mom had a few incredible go-to dishes: beef stew, shepherd's pie, spaghetti with meatballs, and macaroni and cheese chief among them. When she created these dishes, she always used an orange Le Creuset casserole pot to cook and serve in. While the rest of us anxiously awaited its arrival at the dining room table, we'd go through our pre-meal rituals: Dad loading up his plate with salad, then passing it to my brother, while I helped myself to the homemade rolls.

Mom would enter from the kitchen in one of those June Cleaver shirtwaist dresses, carrying the casserole pot with both hands. She'd always head straight for Dad, who was poised for action, serving spoon in hand.

That's when it would start.

Mom would make her way to Dad's left, and he'd begin to heap portions onto his plate with his right hand. Ah, but Dad was left-handed. So why did he use his right hand? And why didn't she stand on his right side so that he could use his natural left?

These were the questions that gripped my mind at the time, and looking over at my brother, it was obvious that I wasn't alone. The two of us looked quite different—Jeff with Mom's blue eyes, light skin, and blonde hair, and me with Dad's brown eyes, dark complexion, and brown hair. And we took our personality cues from opposite parents, too—I was more like Mom and Jeff took after Dad. But in puzzling childhood moments like these, my very different brother and I were often in the same boat.

As Dad served himself, we heard Mom protest in a rather stern, *you are in real trouble now, buster* kind of way, "Mort—stop it." He would freeze, look up to her with a devilish grin, and ask, "What?" His typically booming voice was softer, free of its normal edge, even tender. Mom would shake her head and tell him he was incorrigible. They would both smile, and Dad would finish serving himself before Mom moved on to my brother.

It took me several years to fully grasp what had been going on—I think I was thirteen when I cracked the case. I was burning to tell my brother and did so with haste. Of course, being eleven at the time, the subject was completely out of his depth.

Now, whenever I see an orange Le Creuset casserole pot, my wife, Ginny, smiles, looks directly into my eyes, and says, "Rick, don't you even think about it!"

Saturday Mornings

On Saturday mornings, my brother and I would get up very early—unreasonably early, you might say. We would then steal downstairs, ever so stealthily, so as not to wake up Mom or Dad. Mostly it was Dad we did not want to rouse.

Once downstairs, we'd head to the den and turn on the television. At five thirty in the morning, the only thing on was *The Modern Farmer*. As I think about it today, I guess it was not so modern after all. Times have changed—but I digress.

Like clockwork, we would take our places. Jeff would nestle on the couch and cover himself with the blanket he'd carried downstairs. I would head for the big, overstuffed brown chair (which was really more than a chair, but that's another story), sliding under the autumn-colored quilt that Mom would always place there.

As we settled in, we turned our attention to the man on the screen. In his white shirt and dark skinny tie, he'd break down, for the nation's early risers, the latest cutting-edge techniques for planting saplings or eradicating insects. Of course, we had no clue what he was talking about. But we certainly acted like we did.

But all of this was just prelude, because the main show started at six: *The Mighty Mouse Playhouse.* We loved that mouse and how he would, as the cartoon so accurately claimed, "come to save the day!" We would lose ourselves in his pretend world, where the bad guys were always vanquished and help always came just in the nick of time. A world, I think, that even grown-ups sometimes wish was real.

We would watch our caped rodent hero with the sound turned down so low we could barely hear it, always with an ear out, listening for those footsteps descending from the second floor. I don't think we ever got to see a *Mighty Mouse* episode all the way through, for sure enough, we would eventually hear the dreaded stirrings above.

Frozen into place, we waited as the sound of each step brought our adversary closer to the den.

Clop, clop. On the stairs now.

Clop. Clop. Clop. Louder and closer.

And then . . . the footsteps would stop. Without

looking, we knew Dad was now standing in the doorway. He was not a big man, being of average height and weight. But even with the glasses he wore, we saw him as quite formidable. Especially when that forceful voice of his, tinged with impatience, was directed at us. We knew exactly what he was going to say, too: "What are you boys watching? Turn that junk off now!"

We'd always answer with the same plea: "Daaaad, it's not junk! It's Mighty Mouse, and he's come to save the day!"

Dad would look at us as if we were completely nuts. He'd shake his head, mumble that it was going to rot our brains, and tell us to get dressed. Apparently, there were things to do.

Perhaps if he had awakened earlier and caught us watching *The Modern Farmer*, things would have been different. Dad never did grasp the cosmic import of *Mighty Mouse* . . . or cartoons for that matter.

FALL LEAVES

The fall is often romanticized as a time for strolls in the park, hikes in the woods, the World Series, football, Thanksgiving, and, of course, looking at all the beautiful colors. These autumn traditions held true enough for my brother and me growing up, but all those wonderful colors came with a hefty price tag.

We lived in the country, and trees—large oaks, maples, and pines—surrounded our home. The oaks were most prominent: they covered our property from one end to the other. Of course, in the summer they provided shade and were great for, shall we say, slightly dangerous climbing. It was easier climbing the pines, but then we'd always stain our clothes with pine tar and attract Mom's ire.

But those oak trees—they were something else.

As winter neared, they blanketed the yard in acorns and dead, brown, often soggy leaves. And when Jeff and I were big enough to hold a rake— which, mind you, was when we were half as tall as it was long—we had to rake the leaves into piles and drag them to the woods.

So, on a Saturday morning in the late fall, we would head outside to tackle the chore. The first step was picking a rake. These weren't just any old rakes— they were heavy wooden things with gnarly, claw-like metal fingers that pointed chaotically in all directions. I once suggested to my dad that we get the new light-weight rakes with smooth plastic fingers. Let's just say that I didn't suggest it again.

After picking our tools of the trade, my brother and I would choose a corner of the yard and begrudg-ingly get to it. Before long, we'd start to monitor each other, just to make sure our counterpart was pulling his own weight. Soon enough, when I'd look over at Jeff, he would just be standing there, staring into the woods with the rake in the crook of his arm. I had no idea what he was looking at, but I'd shout at him to get back to work. And, every time, there would be no response. I mean—nothing. He would not move, not even flinch. He just kept gazing into the trees.

Well, I certainly wasn't going to rake the leaves by myself. No sir, not me. I would look down, find the biggest acorn I could, and let it fly.

It's amazing how getting hit in the cheek by a

hard, fast-moving projectile on a cold, windy day can get one's attention. And I always marveled—still do—at just how loudly my brother could wail when my parents were nearby. Sure enough, the noise he made would bring my dad outside in a hurry.

With his first steps out the door, Dad would demand to know what had happened. And, without fail, my brother was more than happy to let him know: for no apparent reason, simply out of the blue, I had heaved an acorn at a defenseless, innocent, hard-working boy.

The accusation now presented to my dad, he would examine the evidence. The red mark on Jeff's cheek made it an open-and-shut case. He would tell my brother to go show his mother; she would take care of it. She could, too—she wasn't just our mom, but a certified nurse.

Then Dad would turn his attention to me, shaking his head in pure disappointment, in that way only a parent can. He'd lay out my sentence: I was to finish the work—all of it. He did not expect to see me until the job was done.

Hours later, sometime in the late afternoon, I would enter the house through the back door, which led right into the kitchen. I would say to no one in particular, "I'm finished." Mom would smile, ask me if I was hungry (knowing the answer), then tell me to get washed up while she made me a sandwich.

As I sat at the table alone with that hard-earned sandwich, I would have a rare moment of clarity. It would dawn on me that I was always finishing the raking job by myself. It was not fair—I was not going to let my brother get away with it again. No way, no how!

But epiphanies can be fleeting. By the time I took my last bite, I would have already decided which acorn—out of the stash I had hidden behind the garage—to use next Saturday morning.

BROWNIE

When my parents brought home the family's new RCA Victor black-and-white television set, they made it clear that it was not to be the center of attention, and as such, it would not be in the living room. That room was for reading the Sunday paper or a good book, entertaining company, and watching the flames flicker in the large brick fireplace.

No, the den was where the television belonged.

The den was added after the house was built. It had a stone-slated floor and long windows spanning the sides. In the far right-hand corner was a glass-paneled door that opened to the outside. The television sat just left of center across from that door, and the curtains behind it were kept drawn so we could see the screen better.

When it came time to get comfortable, there was a little something for everyone: a beige Robsjohn-Gibbings couch of Danish design near the entrance, a black colonial rocking chair by the outside door, and a rather formal wingback armchair in front of the small closet where we stored firewood. But the crown jewel, to me, was to the right of the couch, directly facing the television. It was a chair called Brownie.

This was no ordinary chair. It was an overstuffed club chair, soft and fuzzy and deep chocolate brown. The back was high and rounded at the top, as were the arms. It was so big that two people could nearly fit into it, although my dad assured me it was only for one.

When I was alone in the den—and the Lone Ranger, Roy Rogers, or my favorite, Wild Bill Hickok and Jingles were on TV—that chair was the best horse anyone could have. OK, so it was no Buckshot (Marshall Hickok's horse), but when I threw my leg over the back of old Brownie, the den was transformed into the Wild West.

My mental Wild West was a place where sand and cactus ruled. There was no such thing as a bad guy that I couldn't outride. And with my Mattel Fanner 50 six-gun strapped to my side, there was no one that could outshoot me. Whether standing still or at a full gallop, I was a crack shot. Brownie was fearless, always steady, and never finicky. He never bucked and never tired.

Together we went on too many dangerous adventures to count. (A hero loses track.) Heck, we even rode together through the Civil War, leading the Union Cavalry in a daring raid into the heart of the Confederacy to destroy the railroad line to Vicksburg. You know, like John Wayne did in *The Horse Soldiers*.

To kick off my adventures, I would carefully roll up my blanket and lay it over Brownie, then take a smaller throw blanket and carefully place it on the middle of his back: my saddle. I used one of my dad's belts as a bridle and reins. I was prepared for whatever might lay in wait, be it enemy soldiers, mountain lions, or even grizzly bears. On the trail, you had to be alert for everything. The moment you let your guard down or became careless, you could be seriously hurt or even killed.

Often when I was sick and home from school, I would ride Brownie for the entire day. There wasn't even a need for the television to be on. The house was quiet, as all were out—Mom and Dad at work, my brother in school—and it was just Brownie, me, and my cold. Well, Lassie was there, too (what other name would a young boy give a collie?). Like a pro, she would sometimes run off to our flanks or lag behind to see if we were being followed. But, truth be told, most of the time she was asleep at our feet.

I would stop only to eat the lunch Mom had prepared for me or to drink water from my canteen. Sometimes, I would kick Brownie in the flanks so he'd run like the wind. But other times, I'd lay my head down as I rode, letting Brownie lead the way, so that when I'd wake up we would be at our destination.

As time went by, I noticed he was becoming a bit nicked up, with stuffing showing here and there. And by "stuffing" I of course mean old war wounds and scars from our battles.

One Friday after school, Mom told me she would be busy doing something for Dad, and that my brother had gone to a friend's house. Why didn't I go see what was on TV? Well, that was fine with me.

First I geared up, of course. I changed into my jeans and buckskin jacket, then strapped on my six-gun and went to saddle up my trusty horse. But when I entered the den, I was hit with a shock. In Brownie's usual place sat a modern couch. It had black-and-white stripes and foam-filled pillows.

My Brownie was gone.

I don't know how long I just stood in the doorway, staring at where Brownie should have been. After a while, Lassie came up to my side and nuzzled my hand, as if she knew how lost and helpless I felt.

I sprinted through the house. "Mom! Mom! Where's Brownie? I mean—where's my favorite chair?" When I found her, she smiled, but did not look up, her concentration intently on the papers in front of her. "Your dad and I found a great couch, so we got rid of that old, beat-up thing. The delivery men were nice enough to cart it away."

Mom never looked up. She didn't see how distraught—how lost—I felt in that moment. My

Brownie was gone, and without even a chance to say goodbye.

I walked back to my room in a daze. When I got there, I removed my holster and six-gun and hung them up on the wall. I took off my buckskin jacket and said quietly, "Bye, Brownie." Then I grabbed the basketball from my closest and headed outside to shoot some hoops.

FIRE! FIRE!

It was autumn at 12 College Road, which meant that all around us, summer's cool green leaves had given way to the warmth of orange, red, yellow, and gold. But, as always, the problem was the aftermath.

After several weekends of manual labor with those dastardly rakes (and an occasional acorn assault mixed in), my brother and I had corralled the leaves into piles and carried them to the backwoods. That's when things got really interesting.

Behind the garage, a small way into the woods, my dad had made a clearing. This was where we dumped the leaves and small branches, forming a fairly impressive pile. By the time we were done, it was nearly five feet high and twenty feet across. But that pile was not long for this world.

Dad dragged the garden hose to the edge of the clearing, then watered down the surrounding brush, creating a four-foot-wide wet line that circled the pile. Then he'd start a fire in the corner of it. We would watch as the flames began to lick their way across the top of leaf mound, crackling and popping and sending white smoke up above the trees.

Around the pile, just beyond the line of wet brush, we stood lookout for rogue ashes. If we saw one fly free, we would stomp it out, or my dad would hose down the surrounding area. This was the process we followed, time and again, without fail or incident. That is, until the fall of 1959.

This particular October Sunday began as most did, although I had my best friend Skipper spend the night with me. Mom, Dad, Jeff, Skipper, and I were all sitting around the table having a late breakfast: scrambled eggs, bacon, toast, and orange juice. As we finished up, Dad said that today was the day we'd be burning the leaves. My brother chimed in that the Giants were playing the Eagles that day, and that we'd want to watch it, as it was a big game. Dad smiled knowingly, then said that we'd be able to do both.

After the dishes were done—a team effort—we all headed out back to deal with the leaves. Rakes were handed to everyone. After Skipper and I dragged the garden hose out to the pile, Dad began soaking every-thing around it. We took our positions on the perimeter of the wet brush and Dad lit the leaves on fire.

The pile burned as it always had. White smoke billowed up and we watched for hot embers as Dad continued hosing down the brush. After burning for the better part of an hour, the pile had been transformed into a smoldering black circle. Dad again soaked the area as Skipper and I did a perimeter check. All was in order. Jeff came running up to us, shouting that kickoff was in five minutes. Dad said to leave the hose and rakes where they were and to go get washed up so we could watch the game. He thanked us for our hard work, then said we would pop some corn and maybe get Mom to make hot chocolate.

And so we did. We were enjoying the popcorn and hot chocolate, but we couldn't say the same for the game. The Giants were favored, but they really had their hands full, and I could see that my dad was not happy with how things were going. At the end of the first quarter, Lassie came over to me (as usual when she wanted something) and started whining and nudging my hand. She obviously had to take care of some business, so I got up to let her outside.

When I opened the door I immediately noticed the smoke. It was not just coming from the leaf pile— there was now a line of white smoke snaking its way through the woods. As I looked more closely, I could also see orange flames licking at the undergrowth.

The woods were on fire!

I ran back to the den, yelling for Mom and Dad along the way. By the time I got there, I had their attention. I breathlessly explained the situation.

Dad was the first to get up, but he made it clear that what I said was simply impossible: the fire had almost burned out and he had wet everything down. Even though he was convinced I had to be wrong, he headed to the back door to make sure. Mom beat him there and immediately recognized that it was true. She told my dad to soak the back of the garage, then called the fire department as we boys went outside to aid in the effort.

When we got there, Dad was working the hose full tilt. He told us to never mind the rakes: get more water! We ran back inside, and as Jeff and I topped up two buckets, Skipper filled up a juice glass in the kitchen and dashed outside with it. As I carried the bucket to the woods, Skipper was already running back to the house. I threw the bucket of water at the flames, then headed in to fill it up again—and Skipper sprinted past me once more, another glass of water in hand.

I stopped and watched him incredulously as he tossed his eight ounces of water at the fire, then headed back into the house for more. My mom said to just let him do what he had to. So I did. Jeff and I continued with the buckets, now filling them up from the old water pump in the back yard. It was much faster and water spillage wasn't a big deal outside, unlike in the kitchen.

Soon we heard the sirens of the fire trucks wailing ever closer. One parked on the road and another in the driveway. The firefighters (although in 1959, they were called "firemen") quickly doused the flames and put an end to our little backyard blaze. There was much banter and laughing as Dad chatted up a storm with the fire chief and Mom brought the guys sodas and cookies. (I hadn't even known there were cookies.) Both Mom and Dad let them know how grateful we all were.

Skipper and I even got to stand on the back of one of the fire trucks before they left. As we were getting off, we overheard the firefighters wondering if they would get back in time to see the end of the Giants game.

After we'd all gone back inside, Dad asked Skipper just how many trips he'd made with the water glass. I think it was only then that Skipper realized what he'd been doing. Before he could become too embarrassed, Mom hugged him and thanked him for protecting the house from the fire. As she did this, she gave Dad a look that made it quite clear that not another word should be said about the matter.

After cleaning up, we all headed to the den. The game had just ended. And the Eagles had upset the Giants 49–21, handing them their first loss of the season. My dad shook his head and announced to no one in particular that he was going upstairs to take a shower.

You would think this is where the story ends. You would be wrong.

Just six weeks later, the Giants were sched-uled to play that other dreaded Pennsylvania team, the Pittsburgh Steelers. We were all excited about watching the game that afternoon. At breakfast, Dad announced that, first, we were going to clean up the rest of the leafy mess in the backyard. We would finally burn it once and for all.

My brother and I had, over the prior few weekends, gathered together the burnt leaves and brush from the fire. So Dad, Mom, Jeff, and I (Skipper was not visiting that weekend) again headed for the clearing in back, rakes and garden hose at the ready. Dad was extra careful this time, soaking down a good ten-foot wide swath around the pile.

The second fire burned slowly and steadily, as expected, with white smoke rising through the tree cover into the blue sky. This time, we stayed outside for almost two hours. Finally, when the fire had burned through the pile, leaving only smoldering remains, Dad called it a done deal. "Let's go get cleaned up and watch the Giants destroy those damn Steelers."

My brother was the first one inside the house. As I lagged behind him, I overheard Mom asking Dad if he was sure the fire would no longer be an issue. She suggested that he might want to wet it down again, or better yet, put it out completely. Dad shook his head and said: "That would just make the backyard stink of burnt wet leaves. Who needs to smell that again?"

A little bit later, back in the den, we were watching a real defensive struggle unfold. With the outcome still too close to call, Mom headed to the kitchen to make popcorn.

A minute later, we heard her yelling for my father to get out back, right away. We ran to the kitchen, where Mom was already on the phone with the fire department. Dad actually turned white as he looked out at the woods. Well, he couldn't really see the woods, as they were now shrouded in thick smoke. This time, the fire did not burn east away from the house; the southerly wind burned it north and it ran along the back yard, straight for us. Dad hurried outside to start hosing down the garage.

Within minutes we heard the sirens. A fire truck pulled into the driveway and the firefighters pulled off their hoses and got to work. But, unlike the first time, no one said a word. In businesslike fashion, they hosed down the woods until the fire was out. Then they began packing up their gear.

Not once did they speak to my dad, but I did see several glare at him when they passed him. When they were ready to leave, the fire chief walked over to my dad and unceremoniously handed him a ticket. Dad thanked him, but the chief said nothing as he turned and got into the fire truck.

As I stood watching by the back of the truck, one of the firefighters walked past me. He gave my hair a tussle and said: "Your old man should not be left alone with matches." Then he laughed out loud and climbed up onto the truck. As it was backing out of the driveway, I heard him tell the man next to him: "I hope we make it back for the end of the game this time."

As we walked back into the house, I overheard Mom letting Dad know that they needed to talk. I don't know what they talked about specifically, but Dad never did burn any leaves again. Oh, and the Giants lost that day, 14–9. In fact, the 1959 Giants went 10–2, only losing on the days the Mondschein woods were on fire.

THE SALAD BOWL

Sunday dinners at my parents' table could only be described as major events. Once seated, we could expect to be there for hours. The food was plentiful and it was always really good. My mother had brought the tradition from her family to ours, and it was a seamless transition.

We would usually feast on a roast of some kind, always different, and the leftovers were served all week. If it was a roast beef, we knew we'd be having hash in the days to come. A leg of lamb would become shepherd's pie soon enough. And a pork roast would transform into pulled pork by the following Thursday.

There was always a vegetable. Usually Mom prepared green beans or broccoli, sometimes peas or cauliflower, but never—ever—were Brussels sprouts served at her table. She told my brother and me that she loved us too much to make us endure them. Apparently, she'd had a bad experience with them as a child (but more on that in another story).

But make no mistake: every dinner, no matter the main course, was accompanied by a salad. Not just any salad, and not just served in any bowl—rather the largest wooden bowl I have ever seen, even to this day. It was filled to the brim with lettuce (as many varieties as can be found), quartered tomatoes, cucumbers, red onions, and green peppers, all covered with Italian dressing and plenty of dill.

The bowl was first placed in front of my dad. As soon as we sat down, before the meal was served, he would reach in and carefully steal a tomato, or a green pepper, or on rare occasions, a black olive. During dinner, that salad bowl would be passed around the table several times. Even when the main course was done, and we were sitting there stuffed, Dad would continue picking at the salad. My brother and I would join him until the bowl had been picked bare, the whole process taking the better part of the evening.

Sunday dinner was the time when we shared the events and experiences of the previous week: victories and defeats, test questions we might have missed, trouble we were having with friends. Even the big issues of the day were discussed, from racial injustice, to the space race with the Soviets, to our growing involvement in Vietnam. There was no idle chatter or gossip. Questions and answers flew back and forth across the table between each mouthful of food. Suggestions and guidance were proffered and sometimes, sympathy expressed.

Dad never really discussed the court cases he was working on, but he did join in on everything else. Once, when I was a teen, I made a derogatory remark about President Nixon. Dad put his fork down and looked directly at me. And in a firm, serious voice, stated: "I may be a Democrat, and I may not like what he's doing, but he is the President of the United States. And as such, you will show that office the respect it is due—no matter what you may think of who holds it. Do I make myself clear?"

I assured him that he did.

I know my brother and I would sometimes dread those Sunday dinners. But I learned so much as I sat there and watched my mom and dad interact.

My parents shared the cooking, and in our house, there was no such thing as a woman's or a man's work. My dad did the dishes, cleaned the kitchen, and vacuumed the floors. My mom raked the leaves and shoveled the snow. Of course, as my brother and I got older, we were informed that this was now our work to do.

Dad was my role model, the man whom I most wanted to be like when I grew up (apart from James Bond). So observing him at these dinners was revelatory. I watched him as he listened with real interest, even fascination, to whatever Mom had to say. Whether it was about her day or an opinion about an issue or event, he always wanted to get her perspective. He would actually lean forward when she spoke.

Though I didn't yet grasp the full importance of what I saw, I knew their relationship was different, something I didn't see with my friends' parents or even my aunts and uncles. It wasn't just the obvious love between them. Theirs was a partnership of true equals.

THE SNOW

Looking out at the snowscape, we saw that Mr. White, a client of my dad's, had plowed everything from the driveway to the end of the turnaround, about two-thirds of the way up from the road. It formed the largest snow bank we had ever seen, thirty to forty feet deep.

It was referred to as the Blizzard of 1958. All we knew was that we now had a mountain right in our own yard.

Jeff was the first to begin the ascent to the top and I followed. Climbing was not that difficult, as the snow was packed tightly and our boots did not sink beneath the surface. At the top, we discovered that we were as high as the top of the garage. Even Lassie joined the party, sitting between my brother and me as we surveyed the land around us. Everything was covered in a deep, white blanket.

It was eerily quiet up there, as the snow muffled all the sounds we would normally hear: no chirping of birds, no roaring of cars on the distant road below. Just the occasional whisper of the wind rustling through the pines in the yard, sending snow swirling through the air.

We also quickly learned that standing on top of the snow bank left us vulnerable to the wind and the cold. We decided that we'd be better off at the bottom. It was steep, but getting down the slope was almost as easy as walking up.

Obviously, we couldn't be outside in all that snow and not start making snowballs. The snow was heavy and easy to pack. At first, we decided to see who could throw them the farthest, but that quickly turned to human target practice. We managed, somehow, not to hit each other in the face. So, although our jackets were snow-covered, we were still warm and toasty in our winter gear.

I'm not sure who thought of it first, but before long we were both yelling, "Igloo!" As luck would have it, I had just studied all about Eskimo life in Mrs. Bugbee's third grade class. Jeff, the first grader, only knew what he did from a TV show he'd seen and from what I'd told him.

I explained that we had to build a tunnel entrance that would lead to a big room inside. As the snow bank was already there, we just had to dig it out. Big ice bricks like the Eskimos used would not be necessary.

We made quick work of the entrance. We used the flat snow shovel to take out the snow and form the sides and roof of the tunnel, which we smoothed down with our hands. The snow inside looked almost blue, like you could maybe even see through it. You could not, of course, but it looked that way to us.

We were just about halfway done carving out the igloo's big room when my brother said that he really had to go to the bathroom. And besides, he was cold. I tried to coax him into staying a little longer, but he said he just couldn't wait. I relented, but decided to stay and finish the igloo myself.

Working solo, I not only had to dig the snow out—I also had to remove it. This really slowed me down. I continued carving from the sides and top to expand the room, and then backed out of the tunnel, using my shovel to pull out the loose snow with me.

It was slow work, but the igloo was really coming along. I had made a room in which two people could sit up comfortably and even move around a little. And the tunnel was a proper one, allowing a person to crawl in on their hands and knees without needing to duck. After I smoothed the ceiling with my gloves, I noticed that the room had an even deeper blue tint to it now. It was terrific. I couldn't wait to tell Mom all about it. I scurried out of the tunnel, but then remembered I'd left the shovel.

So I hurried back inside and grabbed it. But instead of turning the shovel so it would easily slide out, I hastily pulled it straight toward me. It wedged into both sides of the tunnel. Frustrated, I lay down and gave it a mighty pull.

Thump! Suddenly I found myself flat on the ground, covered by the snow bank. Buried!

The snow was in my eyes, my mouth, my nose. Breathing was almost impossible. The more I tried to move, the less I actually could. I could only move my feet, and then only slightly, a fruitless wiggle. I also discovered that I could move my hands a little. They were still gripping the shovel and seemed to be uncovered just like my feet. My arms were stretched out in front of me, but no matter how hard I tried, I just could not budge them.

I soon found that with my head turned sideways, almost under my armpit, I could open my eyes and mouth . . . and I could breathe. And that's what I most certainly did.

I started yelling for help, but even as I screamed, I found it difficult to hear myself. I was shivering from the cold and my teeth were chattering. My hands, even under the gloves, were numb. I was beginning to feel very tired.

I don't know how much time went by, lying there like that, but eventually I didn't feel cold anymore. I had stopped shivering. I felt sleepy and thought that if I just took a nap, I would be able to gather myself afterwards and get out of this mess.

As I was closing my eyes, I felt something grab both my feet. Before I could comprehend what was happening, I sensed myself being dragged, pulled, hauled—call it whatever you like. And then I was out of the snow bank, with my mom leaning over me.

She called my name, repeating it over and over again. I remember looking at her and asking, "What?" She started kissing me and cradling me in her arms, rocking me back and forth, and I could see that she was crying. I don't know how long she kept it up, but I finally let her know that I was cold, and she smiled at me and of all things said, "That's great."

Mom helped me to my feet, although I could swear she really was carrying me, and got me into the mudroom where she took off all my snow gear. I wanted to tell her that I could get out of my clothes myself, but I just didn't have the energy. So I watched as she removed everything that was wet. Even my shirt and jeans had been soaked through, which surprised me.

As she was doing this, Mom told my brother to get my bathrobe and a pair of heavy socks—and to do it quickly. "Now, mister. Move!"

It was really strange. I mean, here I was, at the center of the circus, but I felt detached, like I was a spectator watching it all unfold. That is, until I began to warm up. Now I felt terrible. Everything hurt, and I started shivering all over again. All the while, Mom held me and rubbed my hands and feet. She wrapped me up in my bathrobe and put on my socks.

Eventually, things began to improve. Mom helped me to the breakfast table. Within minutes, I had a cup of hot chocolate in front of me, loaded with bite-size marshmallows. She even gave me not one, but three of her homemade oatmeal raisin cookies.

As I dipped the cookies into the hot chocolate (they always tasted best when dipped), I began to feel much better. But as soon as Mom was convinced that I was going to be all right, things began to change. She told my brother to go to his room, and to stay there until she told him to come out. Then she sat down next to me.

And then . . . boy, did she let me have it. "Do you have any idea what could have happened to you? You could have been crushed by all that snow! You could have suffocated or died of hypothermia! Are you listening to me? You could have died!"

She continued: "If I didn't just happen to look out the window and see your little boots sticking out of the snow bank . . . I can't, I just can't, think what that might've meant. Don't you ever do that again! Never!"

Not yet being a hundred percent—not really reading the signs, as they say—I proffered a weak, "But Mom . . ."

"No *buts*, mister! None!"

Having regained enough of my faculties, I saw the error of my ways and gave in: "Yes, Mom. I'm sorry, Mom. It won't happen again, Mom."

9

CHRISTMAS MORNING

The holidays were an interesting time at the Monds-chein residence. Things were a little different in our household, but the season was always full of happiness. Well . . . almost always.

When I was growing up, my dad was Jewish and my mom was a Bahá'í. When we were young, we celebrated Hanukkah: learning about what it meant, lighting candles, giving gifts. My grandma, Dad's mom, would usually join us. It was always a festive occasion.

Mom, being a Bahá'í, had no problem celebrating Hanukkah or any other Jewish holiday. She respected all religions and, Dad being Jewish, it just seemed like the natural thing to do.

We would also celebrate the Bahá'í holy days. A run of them fall between February 26 and March 1, just before the Bahá'í New Year, called *Ayyám-i-Há* ("Days of God") or the Intercalary Days. They are a preparation for the Fast, focused on hospitality, enjoyment, charity, and paying special attention to the plight of the poor and sick. They don't mark any particular event, but the way they are celebrated is, in some ways, similar to the way Christmas is observed worldwide. But Bahá'ís as a practice do not celebrate Christmas.

So with a mother who was a Bahá'í and a father who was Jewish, why am I talking about Christmas? That's easy: my dad believed that every child should celebrate it. Don't get me wrong, he was not referring to the birth of Jesus Christ. He was speaking about Santa Claus and Christmas trees.

At our house, after Hanukkah had ended and the menorah had been put away, a huge candy cane with a big green bow appeared on the front door. Evergreen and blue spruce branches and pinecones decorated the mantle over the fireplace. And when my brother and I were very young, we would, before bedtime on Christmas Eve, put a plate of chocolate chip cookies and a glass of milk on the coffee table in front of the fireplace. That is when Christmas really came alive.

At the crack of dawn, Jeff and I would run into our parents' room and ask if we could go downstairs to see if Santa had come. Mom and Dad would invariably groan and wonder aloud if we could go back to sleep for another hour or so. But they would always relent, laughing as they slipped on their robes and slippers and we pled for them to hurry up.

As we raced downstairs and entered the living room, we could see a warm, colorful glow ahead. When we rounded the corner, there in front of us was a magical sight to behold.

In the corner, near the door leading to the den, was an angel-topped Christmas tree that almost reached the ceiling. Many-colored lights and balls, icicles, and candy canes hung from its branches. Under the tree was a tiny village, and travelling around its base was a locomotive pulling several freight cars.

In front of the fireplace were presents, clearly labeled for the lucky recipients. Hanging from the mantle were five stockings: one for everyone, even Lassie.

You might think that the first thing we did was open the presents. But no, before a single gift was opened, Jeff and I went straight to the coffee table to check on the cookies and milk. Sure enough, there was nothing left but crumbs and an empty glass. And the rug between the coffee table and the fireplace was invariably covered with sooty boot prints running in both directions. My brother and I knew for a fact that Santa had done all of this for us.

Soon thereafter, we would be tearing open presents, then playing with them until we headed off to my parents' friends' house for brunch.

Yes, Christmas Days were always wonderful at our home, among the happiest of my childhood. That is, until I turned nine.

By that time, neither my brother nor I were under the illusion that Santa was responsible for making those mornings what they were. No, we knew that it was Mom and Dad. Mostly Dad, who set up the electric trains and the tree (which we would plant along the perimeter of the yard after the holidays).

Despite our newfound worldliness, that Christmas Eve began the same as all the previous ones. We put out the plate of cookies and milk, although we knew that our parents ate them, and that Dad used his galoshes to make the sooty boot prints. When my brother and I headed to bed, all was right with the world.

Jeff and I shared a room in those days. We awakened at the crack of dawn, as usual. But then we skipped a step. We didn't head for our parents. We just made our way quietly downstairs.

There it all was, in its usual glory: the tree, the train, the empty plate and glass, the presents. We were amazed at just how wonderful it all looked. We could even smell the evergreen and blue spruce branches draped across the mantle. Ironically, it was at this moment that we would forever change Christmas morning.

Caught up in the moment, Jeff and I began to thoughtlessly tear open our presents. And wow, was it a special Christmas. The topper was my Mattel Fanner 50-cap pistol, loaded with "safe-to-shoot" bullets. I even got a real leather belt and holster to put it in. Jeff was also in awe, showing me his new fire engine ladder truck, the exact one he'd asked for. We dumped out our stockings, which yielded new toothbrushes and toothpaste, candy canes, Matchbox cars, and even pencil sets for school. We had gotten everything on our wish lists.

I will never forget the look on Mom's face when she walked into the living room. There we were, in the middle of the floor, with wrapping paper torn and scattered all around us. She put her hand up to her mouth and said forlornly, "Oh, Mort . . ." And then she turned and went back upstairs.

Dad glared at us, shaking his head. After a moment, he said: "I never thought I'd raise two boys who could be so incredibly thoughtless and selfish." And with that, he rejoined my mother.

Mom never did come downstairs that day. Dad had us clean up the mess in the living room, and informed us that we would not be going to Christmas brunch. He also told us that we knew where the cereal and milk were, so we could fix our own breakfasts.

Later in the day, Dad came back downstairs and asked us to sit with him. He let us know how much we had hurt Mom's feelings. He told us that we had deprived her of the joy of seeing our faces light up when entering that magical living room, and of watching our expressions as we opened our gifts.

I can't say that I truly appreciated those words until I had my own children. But after that Christmas, although we always went through the motions and had a great time together, something very special had been lost.

THE SITTER

My parents both worked. Dad practiced criminal law for years before specializing in admiralty and shipping. Mom worked as a nurse-teacher for the Ramapo School District and served as president of the Rockland County League of Women Voters. Between the two of them, there always seemed to be evening functions to attend.

For Jeff and me, this had one important ramification: we often spent those evenings at home with a sitter. Normally we didn't mind, because we thought we had the two best sitters in the world. And they were both guys.

But on one particular night, neither of our regulars were available ... and we got stuck with a girl. Her dad was a well-known actor, and she later followed in his footsteps and became a famous Emmy and Tony Award-winning actress. So there will be no real names given in this tale, to protect the innocent.

And me.

Needless to say, we were not pleased when Mom explained the situation. But our fates were sealed. Our new sitter—let's call her Betty—was already on her way over. When she arrived, I had to admit she was pretty. And she seemed nice. Before my parents left, they made us promise to behave for her.

Why they would be compelled to do such a thing, I can hardly imagine.

Betty told us we could go watch television, and that our parents had given us permission to watch *The Deputy* at nine. But it was straight to bed after that.

Now, that created a problem right from the start, because we wanted to stay up and watch *Have Gun Will Travel* at nine thirty. It was one of my favorite shows, and our normal sitters would always watch it with us. Jeff really didn't care what we watched, as long as he could stay up as long as I did.

While Betty sat at the dining room table doing her homework, Jeff and I headed to the den to watch *Bonanza* (Saturday was western night). As I absorbed the action on that night's episode, a daring and devious plan began to materialize in my mind. I told Jeff that after it was over, we would convince Betty to take a break and join us for a game of cowboys and Indians.

So after the show ended, Jeff went to his room and came out wearing his feathered Indian headdress. I streaked war paint onto our cheeks. (OK, so it was really red marker, but it looked great.) We went into the dining room and told Betty that she was to be our prisoner. She laughed and agreed to a short break.

We told Betty that she had to come with us, then took her to our dad's office space, a study just off the living room. We ordered her to sit in the study's wooden chair, the same one whose hand-carved trees, leaves, and birds had for some reason seemed quite scary when we were younger.

Betty was really a sport about it. She sat down in the prescribed chair, whereupon Jeff and I commenced to tie her up. We fastened her arms and legs to the chair, and even wrapped a rope around her stomach. Then we began whooping and dancing around the room like the Indian braves we had seen on television, and flashing our rubber knives and guns.

This went on for several minutes. Finally, Betty reached her limit and told us that she had to get back to studying. I asked if we could stay up an additional half hour for *Have Gun Will Travel*. She replied that, unfortunately, we could not. Our mom, also known as her employer, had been quite clear when we were to go to bed, and that was at nine thirty.

I asked again, nicely. Even promised that we would go straight to bed when it was over at ten. But Betty held firm. The moment of truth had arrived.

Jeff looked back and forth at the two of us, then

headed somberly for the den. I shook my head, then started to follow him.

"Hey, you forgot to untie me."

I turned to look at her, but Jeff responded first: "No, we didn't."

This seemed to startle our prisoner, who looked at me in bewilderment. I let her know the score. "You're our prisoner now. We'll release you after the show. That's less than an hour from now."

At first, she pleaded with us calmly. But her annoyance soon escalated. She told us that we'd had our fun, and now it was time to untie her. When we did not, to say she became angry would be to understate the case by a large margin. We heard words that even the most grizzled truckers would dare not say.

My brother and I went into the den and closed the door behind us. We watched the end of *The Deputy* and the entire episode of *Have Gun Will Travel*. When they were over, we turned off the television, as promised. As Jeff went upstairs to his room, he let me know that, as it was my plan, I should be the one to untie our prisoner.

When I returned to the study, Betty was sitting there quietly. As I neared her, she began speaking in a voice that was more sad than upset. "I can't believe you boys would do such a thing to me. I just can't believe it." I untied her in silence. Now free, she rubbed her arms and told me to just go to bed, that she didn't want to see or hear from me again.

As I lay in bed, I finally began to regret what we

had done. It also dawned on me that if Betty said anything to Mom or Dad, I would be in serious trouble. As the older brother, it would be me, not Jeff, who would be held to account. Those were my final thoughts before falling asleep.

In the morning, I awoke to the sound of Mom making breakfast in the kitchen. I headed straight for it. Jeff and Dad were there, too, and we all reveled in the smell of frying bacon.

Deciding to get it over with quickly, I asked my parents if they'd had a good time the previous night. Mom said that the dinner party was fun and that the food was excellent. (So far, so good.) With some trepidation, I pressed on, asking if the babysitter had said anything when they got home.

Mom said that Betty had been rather quiet, but related that things went well, and that they had two very interesting boys. Reading into my parents' lack of concern, I could tell that Betty must not have ratted us out. Even if we deserved it. I decided at that moment that no more questions were necessary or even advisable.

I don't know if Mom ever asked Betty to babysit again, but I do know that she never did. The only time I ever saw her after that was, ironically enough, on television. On those occasions, I would always wonder what she thought of her night with the Mondschein boys.

JONATHAN THAD

Jonathan Thad Mondschein is my youngest brother. I never met him. He died only a week after he entered this world on January 8, 1962. He succumbed to pneumonia after having been born prematurely.

I don't recall much about those days, and most of what I do recollect is murky at best. I was eleven at the time, and my brother Jeff was nearly ten.

What I do remember is hearing voices in the middle of the night—anxious, frantic voices. And I remember the blood. I had gone upstairs to my parents' room and saw it on the side of their bed. And it was all over the floor. Mom had apparently hemorrhaged.

I know it sounds far-fetched, but in those days,

when you needed a doctor, they came to your home. My mother's doctor had arrived quickly. He took one look at the situation, and rather than wait for an ambulance, he bundled her in his car and raced to Good Samaritan Hospital.

Dad kept telling us that Mom would be fine, and not to worry. But with Jeff crying, Lassie whimpering, and the fact that the sun hadn't even risen yet, I was scared. There seemed to be a feeling of dread hanging over everything.

At the time, Dad was recovering from detached retina surgery. In 1961 this was not a simple procedure. After the surgery, he had to be kept in the hospital (Presbyterian in New York City), lying on his back, with his head held securely in a fixed position. We would visit him often, but it meant an hour-long car ride each way. After leaving the hospital, Dad had to wear, for several weeks, a metal brace that prevented his head from moving freely.

Mom had been pregnant during this entire stressful period.

Jonathan's premature birth set off a very unsettling and scary time for my brother and me. I don't remember who stayed with us or what we did that week. I don't recall going to school or staying at home. What I do remember is that, for the only time in my childhood, Dad let us sleep with him in his bed while Mom was in the hospital. This was no small thing.

Dad was not one for showing his emotions. He wasn't a hugger, and I don't remember him ever telling me that he loved me until close to the time that he passed. As I grew up, Mom was always assuring me that he did. Perhaps like many men of his generation, Dad believed, or had been taught, that it was not the manly thing to do. I guess I was just supposed to know.

Whatever the case, when I became a dad, I made sure that my children had no doubt. I told them that I loved them often. And I did not spare praise or hugs.

During Mom's hospitalization, Jeff and I were not allowed to visit. "Hospital rules," we were told. Dad was not pleased about this. He argued about it with a large and perpetually scowling nurse, pleading that it would be good for both Mom and us to see each other. But it didn't happen. We were also forbidden from entering the nursery. Jeff and I never got to see our little brother.

Jonathan was laid to rest on January 15, 1962. I've been told that the day they buried him it did not just rain—it poured. Jeff and I didn't attend the burial. Some have told me it was because the weather was so bad.

I don't think that was the real reason. I think Mom and Dad wanted to spare their sons from experiencing a burial at such a young age. I'm not sure that was the correct decision, but it *was* the decision. I also know that Mom didn't attend, either, as she was still in the hospital and would be for several more weeks. It wasn't until much later that I learned just how close we came to losing them both.

I am sure that the loss of Jonathan weighed heavily on my parents. I'm also convinced that it was their faith that got them through it. It gave them a strong belief that, as a baby and a pure soul, my little brother would be all right. And that they would be reunited with him in the hereafter. There are many writings in the Bahá'í Faith (which my dad would eventually convert to) concerning the hereafter, but I would later discover that one in particular was a comfort to them:

> Be not grieved at the death of that infant child, for it is placed in trust for thee before thy Lord in His great Kingdom. Verily God will bestow upon thee that whereby thy heart shall be rejoiced and thy breast shall be dilated. Verily thy Lord is compassionate and merciful![1]

My brother and I never really talked about that time in our lives, and unfortunately, neither he nor my parents are around to discuss it now. I would consider those days every once in a while, but they were fleeting thoughts, and soon replaced with the needs and circumstances of the day. It was not until much later, after I had a family of my own, that I really began to think about Jonathan. And it was not until after I lost Mom, Dad, and Jeff that Jonathan became more central to my thoughts.

---

1. 'Abdu'l-Bahá, *Tablets of 'Abdu'l-Bahá*, Bahá'í Publishing Committee, 1909 ed., p. 730.

When the idea to write this memoir began forming in my mind, I found that I was not only fondly reflecting on Jonathan, but that I actually felt close to him. It may sound strange, but I feel that Jonathan has been encouraging and assisting me with these vignettes. And looking out for his older brother as I continue to stumble along in this plane of existence.

I also believe that, eventually, I will not only be reunited with my parents and Jeff—I will finally get to meet Jonathan, too.

12

THE CAR IN THE DRIVEWAY

It was a Sunday evening in the fall and my parents had gone to a dinner party. At ten and twelve, respectively, my brother and I had made it clear that we most certainly did not need a babysitter for such a short time. We weren't little kids anymore.

Dad was the first to agree with us. And with just a bit more whining and pleading, Mom finally gave in. She said that they wouldn't be out late, as tomorrow was a workday for them and a school day for us. Besides, we should be in bed by ten at the latest. Since *Bonanza* ended then, we could give her that assurance without hesitation.

Sunday was a great television night. First came *Lassie* and *Walt Disney's Wonderful World of Color* (a.k.a.

Walt Disney Presents), then *Car 54, Where Are You?* And finally, my favorite, *Bonanza*, which had been moved from its old Saturday spot. Mom, Jeff, and I typically watched the whole run in the den. Dad thought TV was a waste of time, so he would usually sit in the living room reading the Sunday *New York Times*.

Before leaving, Mom made us hamburgers and hot dogs, which we would pair with hearty helpings of baked beans and potato chips. She even said that, if we were careful, we could eat in front of the television. That was simply *never done* in our house. We were beside ourselves with anticipation.

At seven o'clock, Jeff and I were set up on the floor behind the coffee table, watching *Lassie*. The show now starred Timmy, who was adopted by the Martins after Jeff and his mom, Ellen Miller, had moved to the city. So far, the night had gone according to plan.

As we began eating, I realized that we had forgotten the dill pickles. If we knew anything, it was that one could not eat hamburgers and hot dogs without dill pickles. Since Mom swore by sweet pickles, I think we must have acquired this taste from Dad.

At the first commercial break, I quickly made for the kitchen. We did not have *pause* or *rewind* when we were growing up. Nope, if you missed it, you missed it. So you learned to do whatever you needed to do during the commercials.

As I ran past the open door to my bedroom, I spotted a strange car in the driveway. I stopped in my tracks, then crept into my room and carefully peeked out the window so as not to be seen.

There, in an old, beat-up car, sat a man with a scraggly beard and a baseball cap. I moved away from the window and raced back to the den, letting Jeff know the score. Lassie (ours, not the one on television) let out a low growl, then ran to my room. We followed.

Once there, we saw that the car remained. And just like that, all thoughts of dinner and television were gone.

The sun had already set, and we didn't want this intruder to see us, so we left the lights off and shut my bedroom door behind us. Lassie snarled and tucked her tail between her hind legs. Jeff began petting her, trying to calm her. She licked his face, but kept gazing at the driveway and continuing that low, menacing growl.

All the while, Jeff and I maintained our surreptitious surveillance of the man in the car. We agreed that we had never seen the car or the driver before, though it was getting darker and we couldn't make out his facial features. He lit a cigarette, and each time he took a drag, we saw him silhouetted in the driver's seat. When he finished his smoke, we watched in terror as he swung his car door open. The car light flashed on and he stepped out.

The mystery man was really big. The murky light from the car and the shadows it created made him look ominous. He was wearing what, in the dark, could only be described as scruffy old clothes. Lassie chose that moment to begin growling even louder and baring her teeth.

Not taking any chances, I locked the bedroom door. Then I went over to my gun rack and grabbed two BB guns and loaded them. I gave one to Jeff and kept the other. Then we made a barricade out of bed pillows, blankets, and my desk chair. It stood between the door and the window overlooking the driveway.

Now, of course, in 1962 we didn't have cell phones and there was no telephone in my room. The phone was in the dining room. And that meant it was on the other side of the barricade and the locked door. As such, going for it was not an option. Jeff and I would make our stand here, watching the man in shifts to track his whereabouts at all times.

As it got darker, our situation became bleaker. Before long, we could only vaguely make out the man's silhouette leaning against the car. It was only when he would light another cigarette that we could see his face. And I think we would've preferred not to. He was menacing, what with that unkempt beard and ratty old baseball cap. What made things worse was that every few minutes, Lassie (who was lying on the floor between us) would raise her head, perk up her ears, and emit that guttural growl.

We had been crouched behind the barricade, rifles in hand, for almost two hours. The man was still just leaning against the car and smoking. He was obviously waiting for something—or was it someone? His buddies? His partners in crime? Would they storm the house?

Of course, Jeff and I liberally shared these ideas as we waited. And it was certainly not helping the situation. We formulated numerous horrendous theories, one after the other. Then we heard a car door slam shut.

I carefully raised my head to observe without being seen. And I found that the man was now back in the car.

We could not, for the life of us, figure out what was going on. Why was he in *our* driveway? If he was looking for our parents, wouldn't he have just come to the front door and knocked? If he were lost, wouldn't he do the same thing? But to just stay in the driveway? No, this was not good. Not good at all.

That's when the phone rang. And kept ringing, as there were no answering machines to speak of back then. Jeff and I looked at each other. Could the man hear it? Would he think no one was home? Was it Mom or Dad calling to check up on us? Or one of the man's gang members, checking to see if the house had been secured and the residents dispatched?

Finally, the ringing stopped. Just as the noise had shattered the silence, its abrupt end made it eerily quiet. Too quiet.

As Jeff and I struggled to come up with a plan, Lassie sat up and let out an intense growl—which then turned to a whine as we saw car lights fill the driveway. We heard a car door slam shut . . . and then another. Jeff and I, both shaking in terror, peered out the window.

The man was now standing next to another car . . . and Dad! We couldn't believe our eyes. Then we saw Mom walk over to them. The lights from my parents' car illuminated Dad as he introduced Mom to the man. She shook his hand.

At that point I realized it didn't matter who this guy was, or what was going on. We were safe. But just as quickly, it dawned on me that we had to make Mom and Dad think that all was normal. We had to remove all signs of the barricade. And we needed to act fast.

Jeff threw the pillows and blankets on my bed as I picked up the chair and slid it under my desk. I quickly placed the rifles back on the gun rack. Unloading them would have to wait. As I looked around the room to make sure that all was in order, Jeff and I looked at each other and said in unison, "Dinner!"

We took off for the den. Once there, we scarfed down the hot dogs, which were now cold, and quickly straightened up the coffee table. We rushed into the kitchen with our plates and scraped the remaining burgers, beans, and chips into the garbage (although part of the burgers went to Lassie) and stacked the plates in the sink. All appeared as it should.

We looked at the clock on the wall and saw that it was just turning ten. Not only had we not eaten in front of the television, we had missed all our shows! And we barely got anything to eat. It was already bedtime and we had spent the entire evening behind that makeshift barricade.

Peeking out my window, we watched the man drive off. Jeff and I got up and walked into the kitchen and over to the back door, where we knew my parents would enter. (Only company used the front door.) When they came in, they were laughing.

Jeff raced over and gave Mom a big hug. She was a bit taken aback, but hugged him and told him that she was glad to see us, too. Dad followed Mom in. He rubbed the top of Jeff's head, said hi to Lassie, and petted her side. Then he asked me if everything went OK.

I assured him that everything had. Trying my best to keep my anxiety from showing, I calmly asked him whom he was chatting with in the driveway. He looked at Mom, then back at Jeff and me.

Apparently, the man's name was Mr. Johnson. He was supposed to pick up his daughter at 112 College Road, but he had spilled coffee on the note with the address. So the *112* looked like a *12*. He'd been told that his daughter would be dropped off there sometime tonight, and not to worry if she was late. Assuming that no one was home, he had not bothered to knock on the door.

The mystery now revealed, Jeff and I looked each other over. Although no words were spoken, we both silently acknowledged that, but for the two of us, no one was ever going to know what happened inside the house that evening. Even Lassie seemed to understand.

13

A DISH BEST SERVED COLD

There was a period of time, just before I became a teen, that whenever I was in the den—usually enjoying John Wayne dispatch enemy soldiers, Kirk Douglas secure the West, or Errol Flynn vanquish pirates on the high seas—my brother would walk right in and immediately turn the channel. Usually to a Yankees game.

Inevitably, and nearly every Sunday afternoon, this scene would play out the same way. After Jeff would turn the channel, he would simply sit down. My shock (which diminished the more frequently this occurred) would turn to anger and I would demand that he turn it back to my show. After all, I had been there first.

Having heard my demands, Jeff would just look at me and smile. Then, in a voice sure to reach the ears of our mom, he would cry out: "Rick! Stop hitting me! That hurts!"

I wish I were making this up. But alas, that is exactly what he would say. And like an avenging angel, my mom would come swooping in and demand to know why I had assaulted my helpless little brother.

When she got there, Jeff would be holding his arm and whimpering. It was quite a performance, I'll give him that. I would be told to go to my room.

Oh, the injustice!

Now, when Mom was not there, my brother had a similar ploy, but with a twist. He would come into the room, of course, and turn the channel. But with no parental sympathy to garner, he would walk up and smack *me* on the arm as hard as he could . . . and then run to the hall bathroom and lock the door.

This went on for quite a while, until one day, when the tables of fortune turned. Dad was away on a business trip. Mom had to run to the store, and told me that I should let Jeff know as much when he came inside. I can still remember smiling as I realized all the possibilities this situation presented.

Leaving the Duke to fight the Confederacy without me, I left the den and headed to the hall bathroom.

I went in, closed the door, and locked it behind me. Then, I carefully climbed out the window and walked back into the house and into the den.

I didn't have to wait long. Soon enough, my brother came flying into the room and asked where Mom was. As I told him, he looked at me and grinned a grin that only the wicked can. He walked over to the television and actually said, "See ya, Duke!" Then he switched it to the Yankees–White Sox game, smacked me in the shoulder as hard as he could, and took off for that hall bathroom.

I got up and headed after him, but this time, I did not run in hot pursuit. I walked slowly and deliberately, enjoying each step as I got closer. As I turned the corner and entered that enclosed space with the door to the bathroom dead ahead, there was my brother. He was bent over, whimpering, trying unsuccessfully to open the locked door.

As I approached him, I realized that there was nothing I needed to say or do. I laid my hand on his shoulder, felt him cringe, and said: "I'll leave you to unlocking the door before Mom gets home. You'll have to go through the window." He slowly nodded in agreement.

I returned to the den and flipped the channel back to the Duke, just as he and his men destroyed a railroad and supply depot at Newton Station. After that day, I didn't have to worry about my brother changing the channel. Not without asking me first, of course.

THE GREAT ESCAPE

There were times when I was not well behaved, and my mom would be forced to, shall we say, take certain "corrective measures" in response. On a number of these occasions, more than I care to mention, I would be sent to my room to contemplate my poor decision making. When I really stepped out of line, I would have to spend an entire weekend there, escaping my solitary confinement only for meals.

Once, after giving my parents "lip" one too many times (merely a misunderstanding in my mind), I found myself doing hard time for a third weekend in a row. And the thing is, there are only so many days that you can spend in a single room, even if it's your own room, before going stir-crazy. Especially when you don't agree with your sentence.

I resolved that something had to be done. And that *something*, I decided, did not include approaching Mom and Dad for mercy and forgiveness.

No, what came to mind was inspired by the movie I'd seen about a group of Allied prisoners of war who managed to get away from a supposedly escape-proof Nazi prison camp during World War II: *The Great Escape.* I didn't plan to run away, but I needed to get out of my room on my own terms, even if only for a short time. Like those POWs, I had to come up with a plan.

My parents did not have guards patrolling the perimeter, but they did have my younger brother, Jeff. I knew he would, without hesitation, sound the alarm if I were not in my room. Even Lassie, who was not allowed in my room as I served my sentence, would unknowingly sell me out. She would want to play as soon as she saw me, and that would bring unwanted attention. I also had to make sure that I was present at meal times.

And, so, I would have to serve my time during the day, but nighttime was a different kettle of fish altogether. Jeff would be in bed, and his room was now on the other side of the house. My early-to-bed parents would soon follow, and their room was upstairs (mine was on the first floor). I would make my move in the dark of night.

Outside my room, several tall hemlocks stood. They sheltered my room from the sun, but didn't block the view from any of the windows. Looking out, I could see that the window next to my closet would be my secret exit to freedom.

As this was an older house, the windows were large and wood-framed, with six panels, and they opened vertically. The screens were also wood-framed, and were attached by a male piece on their frames that connected to an eyehook on the windowsill.

Although these kinds of screens made it easy to climb out the window, they made it nearly impossible to climb back in. Nor did it help that the window was about six feet above the ground. Again, this presented no problem dropping down, but getting back in was another story. I had to be able to reach the window so that the screen could be lifted up and away, and there had to be a way to keep the screen pushed out so that I could squeeze through.

As the window overlooked the driveway, all of this had to be accomplished without leaving any evidence that it was being used as an escape hatch. What made this problem more vexing was that I was forced to use only what I had in my room. But if the guys in the prison camp could make do with what they had, I certainly could, too.

I looked to my left, into my closet, and it immediately occurred to me that I could use a clothes hanger. Not the metal ones—they bent too easily. But the wooden ones would work perfectly. They were just long and strong enough to hold the screen away from the window for me to get through, and they gave me the ability to wedge the screen open from the outside using the end of the hook. They were also small enough to stow out of sight once I was outside. The whole operation would be tricky, but I was up for it.

Now it was just a matter of time.

In the evening, my brother called me to dinner. When I got to the table, Dad asked Jeff what his plans were for the next day. Jeff looked at me with a smile and said: "Well, unlike Rick, I'll be going over to a friend's house to shoot hoops." Mom was not amused, and told him that if he didn't behave, he wouldn't be going anywhere either. As my parents turned the conversation to current events, I didn't pay much attention. I just ate in silence, and every once in a while gave my brother a look that promised he would have his comeuppance soon enough.

When dinner was done, Mom sent me back to my room. Now all I had to do was wait patiently for everyone to go to bed. Mom always enjoyed watching *The Defenders* on Saturday nights, which ran from nine to ten. I knew she'd be heading upstairs after it was over, and that the coast should be clear after that.

Sure enough, just after ten, there was a knock on my door. Mom came in and let me know that Dad was already upstairs and that she was going to bed, too. She also told me it was time to turn off my light and to follow suit. Already under the covers, I nodded in agreement. She kissed me on the forehead, then said that she loved me despite not being happy with me at the moment. I nodded, then turned toward the wall. She switched off the light, said good night, and shut the door behind her as she left.

A few minutes later, through my windows, I saw the outside lights go out, throwing the driveway and my room into darkness. I tossed off the covers and sat up, then reached under the bed for my sneakers. I had been fully dressed the whole time and Mom had been none the wiser. I crept over to my door and listened. All was quiet.

I figured that Jeff and Dad were already asleep, and that Mom would join them within ten or fifteen minutes. I sat on my bed and waited, staring at the clock. I don't think I ever really appreciated just how long ten minutes was until that night.

After what seemed like forever, the clock finally flipped to 10:20 p.m. I put another ear to the door. Not a peep.

I moved over to the window and quietly opened it. I unlatched the screen and it easily swung away from the windowsill. I let it fall quietly back into place, then went to grab a wooden hanger from the closet. I returned to the window, pushed the screen back out, and wedged the hanger between the sill and the screen on the left-hand side of the window. This provided an opening of about twenty inches. It would be tight, and the going would be slow, but it would work. And it did.

I crept out and hung above the ground by my hands, then let myself drop. It wasn't far at all. I jumped up and grabbed the hanger, pulling it down, and the screen thumped back into place. I reached up with the hanger and gave the screen a slight push, leaving a little gap so I could nudge it back open. I decided not to tempt fate by testing it; trying once, when I returned, would be enough. I hid the hanger behind the closest hemlock.

I had done it! The escape had gone off without a hitch. As a free man, I stood on the driveway and surveyed my surroundings. I had to admit it was really dark, since both the outdoor and indoor lights were off. I could barely make out the garage. It was overcast, too, which prevented even the moonlight from helping.

I slowly walked to the garage and, finding Mom's Plymouth Valiant, I sat on the rear fin. OK—I was out, but now what? Apart from the near-zero visibility, I hadn't bothered to wear a jacket. And it was chilly.

So, I decided, I had proven my point. I now had a secret way out of my room and I could come and go on my own terms. I'd best get back and regroup.

Suddenly, lightning ripped away the darkness. A jolting thunderclap followed almost immediately, shaking the garage and the car. It scared the heck out of me.

My first thought was that the noise certainly woke up everyone in the house. I had to hope my parents wouldn't come downstairs to reassure us that all was well. My second thought was that it was almost a sure bet that Jeff would fly up the stairs to their room. He hated the thunder—almost as much as Lassie did.

Lassie! Her deep fear of thunderstorms would often compel her to head for cover under my bed. But my door was shut, so she was probably climbing the stairs alongside Jeff, hoping to get under Mom and Dad's bed.

I hurried to my window and found the hanger behind the hemlock. As I was reaching up to unhook the screen, another bolt of lightning lit up the sky, the side of the house, and my window. It also revealed my mom's face on the other side of the screen.

What I remember most were her eyes. In them I saw relief, anger, frustration, and disappointment. At that moment I wanted to be anywhere other than where I was, standing in front of her.

Another loud clap of thunder made me jump. Mom shouted through the screen: "Get your butt to the back door right this minute, buster! It's dangerous out there!"

I turned and tore up the driveway. That's when the heavens opened up.

It was as if a huge bucket of water had been dumped on my head. One moment I was dry, and the next I was soaked to the bone. Mixed in with the rain were hailstones that painfully pelted my skin. I kept running as the lightning showed me the way. When I got to the door, Dad was standing there. He wordlessly shook his head and headed back upstairs. I grabbed a towel from the bathroom and went to my room.

I found Mom sitting on my bed. As I dried my

hair, she told me to sit down next to her. After a moment, she asked: "What will it take to get you to stop this defiant behavior and to straighten up and fly right?"

I couldn't face her. I just stared at the floor. She grabbed hold of my chin and turned my face toward her. "Eric, we do so love you. But what are we going to do with you?"

Now, in those days, everyone called me Rick. And my parents often called me Ricky. But when they were at their wits' end with me, I was called by my real name, Eric. This was clearly one of those times.

Mom stood up. "What possessed you to go out the window, anyway?"

I told her that I wasn't sure, but that seeing *The Great Escape* had somehow compelled me to make a break for it.

She actually laughed. Her face took on a kind of Cheshire cat smile as she said: "Well, young man, perhaps you forgot how the movie ended."

I wasn't sure I was following, and I think she sensed my confusion. Very slowly she helped me to stand up. She looked directly into my eyes, like she was peering into my soul. "Most of the prisoners were recaptured by the Nazis and executed."

With that, she turned on her heels and walked out of my room, closing the door behind her.

GOING FOR THE GOLD

In early 1964, the Winter Olympics were held in Innsbruck, Austria. My brother and I were glued to the television, cheering on the USA. It was quite disheartening to see us come up short time after time, while other countries took home the lion's share of the medals. The Soviet Union took the most gold and won more medals than any other nation. We did win a few, but none in the two-man bobsled competition.

No, the gold in that prestigious event went to the British (who insisted on calling it a *bobsleigh*) and the silver and bronze medals went to the Italians. When we witnessed the American bobsled team come in seventh, Jeff and I just knew we had to do something about it. We could not let this stand.

As we listened to "God Save the Queen," my brother and I resolved to beat the Brits ourselves. He and I would soon be standing on that medal platform with the Stars and Stripes flying and the "Star-Spangled Banner" ringing out. It was a matter of personal and national honor.

So began the arduous task of determining how we could unseat the Brits. For starters, we needed a bobsled. (There was no way we were going to ride a *bobsleigh*.) We had snow saucers, but those were designed for only one person. They were not sleds in any way, shape, or form. So right away, we were stumped. We couldn't come up with anything that would work.

So we decided to take a break and get something to eat. On this particular day, we had to make our own lunch, as Mom and Dad had gone into the city to attend an event with one of Dad's clients. It always amazes me how so many of our best ideas can be found when we stop looking for them. And sure enough, as we walked into the kitchen, there on the floor in front of us was the plastic runner. My mom had put it down on the floor to keep us from tracking mud or snow throughout the house. We both saw it at the same time, and almost in unison, we shouted, "It's perfect!" And it was. It was five feet long and almost two feet wide. Never mind the fact that it was see-through, thin, and incredibly pliable. It was a bobsled, no doubt about it.

Now we needed to find a course—something built

for speed. Unfortunately, there was little snow in the yard. The driveway had been plowed and was bone dry. Disappointed, we came in and removed our jackets and shoes. As we headed through the kitchen to the hall, we looked to our right. And there in front of us was the ultimate bobsled course: the stairs leading to the second floor. Of course!

The stairs were carpeted. At the top they banked hard to the left. All right, so they did not really *bank*, so much as make a ninety-degree turn to the left before the final five steps to the second floor hallway. And there was another hard left turn near the bottom. Kind of like an inverted *U* shape, but with straight lines rather than curved ones. With a couple of Mom's long and squishy bolster pillows, Jeff and I agreed that we could transform those hard turns into banking curves. Yep, this would make a world-class Olympic bobsled course, all right.

Next we had to design our uniforms. We decided that a simple white T-shirt with the letters *USA* in blue on the front and back would be perfect. We did not want to use the color red, as that was too, well, *Soviet*. So, with the help of a blue marker and an alphabet stencil, we had our custom USA gear.

We also agreed that, like the members of all Olympic bobsled teams, we had to wear helmets. Luckily, we both had football helmets with faceguards. They were white with a blue stripe down the middle. We used our markers to stencil *USA* across the back of each helmet. Beautiful. We also agreed that we would wear our snow gloves to protect our hands as we made the run down the course. After all, we would need to hold onto to the edges of the runner—er, bobsled.

We created what we thought was a great banking turn using Mom's two bolster pillows, which we liberated from the den couch. We stacked them on top of each other in the corner on the landing, where the upper set of steps met the stairs heading to the first floor. It was the final curve, or, in bobsled racing terms, the "Finish Curve."

Next, we turned to the problem of the landing at the bottom of the course. It looked to be a little rough. Jeff came up with the idea of taking the pillows from every bed in the house: twelve in all. We piled them up evenly at the base of the stairs. As far as we were concerned, we now had our safe landing area.

As Mom and Dad would be getting home at any moment, we regretfully determined that we'd have to wait until they were away again to make our run to glory. And, sure enough, the next Saturday we found ourselves with our opportunity.

First, we decked ourselves out in our full uniforms: T-shirts, gloves, and helmets. There was no question that we represented the USA. We placed the two bolsters so as to make that banking Finish Curve and arranged our pillowed landing.

Go time.

Standing at the top of the course, it looked pretty challenging. We felt it would be a good idea to have a trial run with the unmanned sled, just like at the

Olympics. So we took the plastic runner/bobsled and, each one holding a side, we started rocking it back and forth. We had watched the Olympic teams do this to allow for maximum takeoff speed.

On the count of *three*, we sent the sled flying down the first flight of stairs. We watched in awe as it banked the Finish Curve in fine form before careening down the final part of the course and coming to a quick stop in the landing area. We jumped up and down in triumph. We could already feel the hefty gold medals hanging around our necks.

Ordinarily, the bigger team member rides in the back, so he can provide a heftier push-off while the smaller one steers from the front. But, as I was the oldest, I demanded to be in front. We laid the bobsled down with the front hanging just over the edge of the top stair. Then we took our places and grabbed hold of the edges of the sled, lifting them up in the air.

We started rocking the sled back and forth, inching toward the course until we finally reached that critical point. The fulcrum point. And we began to slide forward.

Now, I'm not sure if we both came to the conclusion that this was not a good idea at the same time, but I am quite sure we both realized as much during that first leg of the run, just before we hit the Finish Curve. We banked as expected through the turn, but as we picked up speed we found that we had made a horrible, catastrophic mistake.

As it turns out, there was a flaw in our engineering. You see, the stairway did not open onto a foyer. Rather, the stairs began from a hallway that ran horizontal to the steps. The bottom step was a mere thirty-eight inches (just shy of a meter in Olympic terms) from the wall. There is no way of stopping a plastic runner sailing full speed down the stairs in thirty-eight inches.

I would like to tell you that when the sled hit the pillows at the bottom of the course, we came to a nice, pillowy stop. But I can't. We did come to a stop, but it was rather abrupt. After sliding with incredible speed down the bottom of the course and sailing over the tops of the pillows in the landing area, we came face-to-face with the wall.

I do not say "face-to-face" lightly. I was propelled head-first into the wall, followed closely and above me by my brother. It's true what some have said about being in an accident. Everything seems to slow down and you become aware of nearly everything around you.

As we raced over the pillows, I saw Lassie, out of the corner of my eye, run in the opposite direction. Like she knew this wasn't going to end well and wanted no part of it. I also saw the wall coming toward me rather quickly. Then I heard a loud *thud*, *pop*, and *crackle*—and my brother fell on top of me.

After an impossibly long couple of seconds, Jeff rolled off of me. We sat up, asking each other if we were all right. Still in a daze, we noticed there was a lot of chalky dust in the air. We turned and looked at the wall that had stopped us.

Well, what was left of the wall, anyway. Staring right at us were two huge indentations. Our helmets (and us landing between the studs) had apparently saved us from severe injury and at the same time caused serious damage to the drywall. I reached into one of the jagged, cracked dents and tried to pull it back into shape. All I accomplished was tearing out a rather large piece.

My brother looked at the wall, then at me, then at the piece of drywall in my hand. Dejectedly, he offered: "I guess this means we don't qualify for a medal."

We both recognized that when Mom and Dad got home, things were not going to go well for us. And to top it off, the British still had the gold.

THE PARACHUTE JUMP

A split-rail fence ran around three sides of our yard. It traced the road in the front of the house and ran a short way into the woods on the north side. There was no need for a fence along the southern perimeter. There, after a small patch of thick woods, was a hurricane fence that guarded the top of a cliff. Several hundred feet below was the New York State Thruway.

We also had a couple of sheds. The one farthest from the garage was used to store posts and rails for the fence. The one next to the garage was our playhouse. It had a sloped roof that was nearly twelve feet high on one side, but slanted down to about ten feet on the other. My brother and I had built a ladder up the side of the shed that faced the woods in the back.

We often climbed up on the roof, as it made a great lookout post.

After seeing *The Longest Day*, the shed roof became much more than just a lookout post. It was now an airplane. Not just any kind of plane, mind you, but a Douglas C-47 Skytrain. And we were US Army paratroopers.

Before launching ourselves off the west side (and into the soft grass of our side yard), we had to figure out what we could use for a parachute. We knew from watching cartoons that a large umbrella was probably the best bet—just like Dad's old one. Granted, it was black, and everyone knows that parachutes are white. But we figured that if we did a nighttime jump it would be like having a real, camouflaged nighttime chute. We both wondered why the army didn't use black chutes for night jumps.

One Saturday afternoon, after Mom and Dad had left to run some errands, Jeff and I decided it was time to make the drop. We dressed in our army outfits and strapped on our side arms and canteens. Perhaps recalling the experience of our bobsled run, we agreed that wearing our football helmets would be a good idea. We could always think of them as army helmets.

Armed with the old umbrella, we climbed up onto the roof. Jeff said that he should go first. Considering what we were about to do, I figured: why not? Better him than me. We sat on the corner of the roof and proceeded to fly our plane to an altitude of about ten thousand feet. As I kept the nose into the wind, I told Jeff, who stood at the edge of the roof, that we were over the "LZ" and he should jump any time now. He confirmed the order, then leaped out into the sky. And just like in the movie, he yelled, "Geronimoooo!"

It is surprising how quickly one can close ten feet when falling. In fact, I don't believe Jeff even finished his battle cry before he hit the ground. What I do know is that just as he launched himself off the shed, the umbrella turned inside out and was of no use at all.

Amazingly, Jeff was not hurt, although I think he was in shock. He didn't think the umbrella made a good parachute, and I couldn't really disagree. After some pondering, I came up with a great Plan B. I told Jeff to wait there; I would be right back.

I climbed down the ladder (I wasn't going to jump in these conditions) and ran to the garage. And there it was. Leaning against the wall was the umbrella for the picnic table. It came in two pieces and was rather large and heavy. Still, I managed to carry it over to the shed. I told Jeff that this would make the perfect parachute, as when it opened it was almost as big as a real one.

I climbed up onto the roof. Jeff handed the end of the umbrella to me and I pulled it up there with me. Jeff got "on board" and together we cranked the umbrella open. It was big, all right. When it was open it seemed to span the whole roof.

It was my turn now. I moved over to the ledge and,

holding the picnic table umbrella in front of me with both hands, I leaped into the air. In that incredibly brief jump I learned that with the umbrella open—and it did stay open—I couldn't hold on to it. So I fell like a rock, while the umbrella floated down a short distance away from me. I was a bit rattled from my helmet hitting the ground and my subsequent roll, but I was OK.

Now we were faced with another engineering problem: how to maintain control of the umbrella during the jump. As usual, the "perfect" idea came to me. If we simply duct taped the umbrella to my hands, I could hold it all the way down to the ground. Problem solved.

Jeff got the duct tape. Just when we were going to start taping my hands, we saw Mom and Dad pull into the driveway. We laid the umbrella down on the shed roof and climbed down. We greeted them, then helped get the groceries into the kitchen. Our duties thus fulfilled, Mom thanked us and told us to go play. She would call us when dinner was ready. Without hesitation we were out the door.

We returned to the shed roof. And without really pausing to think about what we were doing, we fastened my hands to the umbrella pole. But with my hands taped to the pole, Jeff would have to muster the strength to crank the umbrella open. Somehow, he did just that. We made our way to the roof's edge. The umbrella was wide open and difficult to keep steady. A late afternoon breeze began blowing in from the west.

We realized that if Mom looked out the breakfast nook windows she could easily see what we were doing. Worse than that, if Dad were helping her to set the table, which he always did when he was home, he could see us, too. Not good.

Not ones to be easily thwarted, Jeff and I decided that I would just have to make the jump from the other end of the shed, into the woods. So with the wind at my back and with Jeff having cranked open the umbrella, I took two steps and launched myself into the air. For a moment, I seemed to just hang there. It was working! But just as I was about to let Jeff know as much, I heard and then saw the umbrella begin to collapse inside out. And I fell like a rock.

Unlike on the other side of the shed, there was no grass to land on where I had leaped. Only rocks, branches, and thorns awaited me. With the picnic umbrella duct taped to my hands, I couldn't even fend off any of the branches as I fell through them.

I hit the ground hard and tried to roll like the paratroopers in *The Longest Day*. But the umbrella pole dug into the ground and pirouetted to the right, dragging me along until it came to an abrupt stop. It was now lying across my chest and face, wedged into the tree I had just missed when landing.

I could hear my brother asking me whether or not I was OK. I think just hearing him ask the question made me relax a little. I was actually laughing as I reminded him of the phrase from the movie: "any landing you can walk away from is a good one." But then I realized that I couldn't get up. The umbrella had me pinned to the ground, and my right foot was beginning to throb. It also felt wet, which was curious, since the woods were as dry as could be.

Jeff was the first to notice. I watched the color drain from his face as he pointed down at my foot. I told him I couldn't see it with the umbrella pinning me down. Luckily, he remembered my pocketknife. He fished it out of my pocket and cut the tape off my hands.

I was having trouble standing. I managed to get up with Jeff's help, but I felt like I was wearing a ski on my right foot. And, sure enough, that's exactly what it looked like, too. A piece of wood, about three feet long, was stuck to the bottom of my sneaker. I tried to shake it off, but to no avail. Jeff stopped me, pointing again at my foot. I wasn't really aware of what he was pointing at until he told me in a rather weak voice to look at my sneaker. I did. And what I saw made me immediately dizzy and sick to my stomach.

There, sticking out of the top of my sneaker, was the pointy end of a huge nail. And, let's face it, in order for a nail to be sticking through the top of my shoe, it had to have entered the bottom and passed through my entire foot. And that it had, after traveling through a two-by-four piece of wood.

I broke into a cold sweat. Not only was my foot really beginning to hurt, but there was no way we would be able to keep this from Mom and Dad.

With Jeff's help, I walked toward the house. Well, a better way to describe it would be "waddling," as with a swim flipper. With every step, I had to lift my foot high enough to drag the almost three-foot-long board up and around. Each step made a *clopping* sound as the wood slapped the ground. The only good thing was that we couldn't see much blood, because the nail was plugging both the entrance and exit wounds.

Jeff opened the back door and yelled for Mom as we stepped into the mudroom. Walking in was no problem, but trying to climb the steps in my condition was not easy. I recall yelping as I pulled my boarded foot up each step. My mom arrived, and with one look, assessed the situation in its entirety. She had me sit right there on the kitchen floor.

As a former navy and emergency room nurse, Mom had seen worse. She acted like it was no big deal, maybe just to keep me calm. But when my dad entered the kitchen and saw the state of affairs, he turned as white as a ghost. Mom jumped up and helped him as he literally slid down the refrigerator until he was sitting on the floor across from me.

Mom told him, in an even tone: "Mort. Just look out the window and do not look at Rick. He'll be fine. Just look out the window."

As Mom evaluated my foot, she asked my brother to explain how this unfortunate scenario came to pass. I thought it would've been more than sufficient to indicate that I'd inadvertently stepped on the board. But, no; Jeff was all too willing to explain the entire event, from start to finish. No detail was spared.

Judging from the facial expressions cascading across my mom's face, I could see that she was neither amused nor impressed. She said she'd have to take me to the emergency room to have the nail removed. I would also need both a tetanus and a penicillin shot as a preventive measure. I heard her assuring both Dad and Jeff that after the doctors saw me she would bring me home later that day.

I don't recall the ride to the hospital. But I do remember my mom staying with me as the doctor and nurses removed the nail and board from my foot. And yes, it hurt. A lot. Even though I was lying down and looking away, I couldn't help but see the bloody gauze pads piling up as they worked.

My mom held my hand the whole time they worked on me. She kept saying there was nothing to worry about, that she had seen much worse. It calmed me down, no doubt. And I was still all right when the nurse gave me the tetanus shot in my arm. But Mom's calming words were quickly forgotten when I saw the size of the needle the doctor was going to use on my foot.

I will never forget that shot. The pain was incredibly intense, and for a while afterwards, my foot felt like it was on fire. But I also remember the pain pills they prescribed. After taking them, although my foot still hurt, I didn't much care.

My mishap caused me to miss several days of school. I spent most of that time laid up on the couch in the den watching television. Mom and Dad never acted like they were mad at us for jumping off the shed roof. I guess they figured that neither one of us would do it again.

They were right.

MOM'S IN THE KITCHEN

"Rick! Careful! Those pots are hot! The last thing we need is for you to get scalded!"

Such is how Mom would typically greet me when I "bounded," as she claimed, into the kitchen. Perhaps I was walking rather quickly, but when those incredible aromas wafted through the house, I just had to get to the source.

Even though Mom worked full-time, when berries were in season she could often be found in the kitchen baking pies and making preserves. Which gave me the chance to spend some real time with her.

It was a heck of an operation. Mom would have large pots boiling on the stove as she sterilized Mason jars and melted paraffin. Strewn all over the kitchen

counters were bowls filled with raspberries and blue-
berries. Cutting boards would be piled high with
sliced apples and peaches. And the breakfast table
was covered in wax paper, so that Mom could roll out
the pie crust dough.

She always wore a white apron. Flour on her
forehead and chin betrayed where she had rubbed
her face, and berry stains covered the front of her
apron. I would stand and watch her move with
catlike precision from one end of the kitchen to the
other: preparing the berries and fruit, rolling the
dough, checking on the Mason jars, and ensuring the
paraffin was doing whatever paraffin does.

Even while conducting this chaotic symphony,
Mom would always find a way to talk with me. Most
often we found ourselves alone, with Dad and Jeff
otherwise occupied or simply avoiding the kitchen.
But I relished these times. She and I talked about
anything and everything. I would sit there and listen
contentedly while swiping berries at will.

Mom would sometimes tell me about her being
a tomboy. That she didn't play with the other girls
much when she was little, and didn't like playing with
dolls or having tea parties. She preferred playing tag,
climbing trees, and going fishing. Things the boys did.

Once, she stopped in the middle of cutting up
an apple, a thought having hit her. She smiled and
told me about the time she went to see *Tarzan*. After
the movie, she and her friends went to the park and
began playing the jungle warrior, climbing trees and

swinging from one branch to another. Mom climbed one of the taller trees and leaped toward a branch that was just out of her reach. She plunged to the ground and broke her arm in the fall, and had to wear a cast for the rest of the summer.

I could relate.

Besides her adventures, Mom also let me know that life at her childhood home wasn't always pleasant. She never went into much detail, but she did give me a glimpse. She told me that her mom did not brook bad manners. That when you sat at the table, your left hand had better be in your lap while you used your fork with your right, except when you had to use your knife. And once, after being warned several times about putting her elbow on the table, her mother had tied her left arm to the chair. I was glad that practice wasn't continued in our home.

Another time, she refused to eat her Brussels sprouts. Her mother ordered her to stay at the table until she did. It wasn't until the middle of the night that she was finally excused to her room. In the morning, they were again put on her plate. I imagine this might be the reason Mom never served Brussels sprouts in our house.

Mom also used these opportunities to tell me a little about my dad. He did not talk about growing up, and whenever such personal matters came up, he always seemed to change the subject. But through Mom, I learned that Dad's father had died when he was young. He and his older brother, my Uncle Jerry, had to support his family during the Great Depression. My dad sold newspapers as a young child in Brooklyn, and later, shoes. He continued to support his mom while he went to college and law school.

Mom smiled as she related that Dad once raised and flew pigeons, often sending them up to lure other flocks to his coop. I recall asking her, "But wasn't that really stealing?" She laughed. "I suppose so, in a way. Might explain why your dad went to law school." Then she got quite serious. "Your father may put up with a lot, but he does not tolerate stealing, lying, or hurting others. Especially those who cannot protect or defend themselves."

I would be remiss if I did not point out that during the entire time Mom was talking to me and baking, she smoked. That's right, she smoked cigarettes, and not just any kind, either: unfiltered Chesterfields. She smoked almost two packs a day, and in almost all my recollections of her I can still see a cigarette in her hand, just like most of her generation. After all, "nine out of ten doctors" approved (at least in magazine ads), and countless Hollywood greats did it, too.

Even my dad smoked—but I never knew it until my wife and I saw him smoking at our wedding reception. He apparently only smoked at the office and never at home. I now have a better understanding of why he could always be found chewing Chiclets gum.

Sometimes, Mom used those occasions in the kitchen to share her thoughts on matters she felt were simply important for me to know. She would, for example, talk about the importance of always being truthful, and of understanding that girls and women were my equals. She would say that trust would form the foundation of every relationship I would ever have, and that only by working in partnership would any of my relationships flourish and grow. This was an issue of great import to her, and to my dad. She got no argument from me. Watching how my parents interacted and supported each other, it just made sense.

Taking that conversation a step further, Mom also never failed to let me know how I must never, and I do mean never, do *anything* after a woman said "no." At this point in the conversation, I would raise my hands and plead that I understood, then try my best to change the subject.

These sessions had one other benefit, and a nearly miraculous one at that: they actually managed to convey to me the importance of math and science. Who cared about fractions or chemical compounds, anyway? No matter how often my teachers tried to explain why I should, I would simply tune out. But after watching what Mom had to do to make those incredibly delicious pies and preserves, I finally understood.

ONLY THE VALIANT

My parents owned a blue-and-white 1956 Chevy Nomad station wagon. In 1960, however, my dad said he was no longer interested in, to paraphrase Dinah Shore, seeing the USA in his Chevrolet. So, one day, my parents came home with a black, four-door, 1960 V-200 Plymouth Valiant.

Its red interior boasted checked cloth bench seats, front and back. They were patterned in a brocade style, and highlighted with fine metallic threading and grained vinyl borders. Even the dashboard was red.

The car kind of looked like a jet fighter to me. It had a fuselage shape and distinct blades above the dual headlights that extended horizontally, over the front wheel and onto the front door. A similar formation began low on the body and arched up over the rear wheel, continuing toward the slanted, cat's-eye taillights. With its sculpted sides, Dad said it was rather a "loud" design. I must say the Valiant didn't look like any other car on the road. Some loved it and others hated it.

Mom disagreed with Dad about the appearance; she said it was rather "European" or "Continental" looking. Needless to say, Mom drove the Valiant most of the time. Dad would take his green 1953 Oldsmobile 88 to the train station every day. He said it was reliable enough to get him wherever he needed to go, but I think he just didn't want to be seen driving the Valiant.

Perhaps the most unique feature of the Valiant was that to shift, you merely had to push a button. The shifting buttons were located to the left of the steering wheel and lined up vertically: *reverse*, *neutral*, *drive*, *second*, and, at the bottom, *first*. It also had a switch for putting the car in park.

I was enthralled with the idea of just pushing a button and driving away. I would often climb into the driver's seat when the car was parked in the garage and pretend to drive. I'd push the buttons from first to second to drive, imagining I was navigating a racecar or a rocket.

As I got older, I realized that I might be able to actually drive the Valiant someday. Mom promised that when I was old enough, she'd let me use it. Of course, I had to be sixteen first, then make it through driver's ed for my learner's permit. And that was still three years away. But even at thirteen, I knew that car and I were destined to be together. I knew it in my bones.

One warm and sunny June Saturday, Mom left with a close friend to go shopping. Shortly afterwards, Dad departed as well, to go help a friend with a legal problem. Given the option, he took the Oldsmobile, of course.

My brother had a friend over and they were playing catch in the side yard. They asked me if I wanted to join them, but I told them I wasn't in the mood and headed inside to check out what was on TV. Walking through the living room, I spotted, laying right on the coffee table, the keys to the Valiant. There was no mistaking them. There were two keys on a ring: one for the ignition and the other for the trunk. They were attached to a black leather key fob. On it was a medallion, with the word *Valiant* scripted in bright silver letters over a light yellow circle and a red-and-blue arrowhead.

The keys weren't just sitting there. They were calling me, beckoning me, challenging me.

There was no way I could turn down such a challenge. I picked up the keys and held them in my hand. I could feel the smooth medallion surface and the raised lettering. I knew what I had to do, and yet I also knew what I could not do. I wasn't out of my mind: I knew I couldn't take the car out for a spin. To do so could jeopardize my ability to ever drive if the police caught me. So I set my sights just a little lower.

I headed for the garage. It was detached, but painted white and fitted with the same black-shingled roof and clapboard sides as the house. Although it could fit two cars comfortably, it only had one door. But that door was huge and it was heavy. It was made of wood and had a row of windows along the top. Once you began lifting it up, it had big springs which helped you complete the job, and subsequently held the door in place.

The garage held a lot more than our two cars. Joining the automobiles were our bikes, all manner of lawn equipment and outdoor tools, Mom's garden supplies, snow tires, spooled hoses, countless boxes and bottles, and my dad's cluttered workbench. It had curtained windows on both side walls, a shelf that sat high along the back wall, and an attic that ran the entire length and width of the garage.

I entered and climbed right into the Valiant's driver's seat. There was no harm in just putting the keys in the ignition. No harm at all. I might have only been thirteen, almost fourteen, but I had watched Mom and Dad drive and I knew how this was done. I slid the key into place and turned it to the right while gently pushing down on the gas pedal. The car started right up. I removed my foot from the pedal and just listened to the engine *purr*.

It was time to get comfortable. I adjusted the mirrors and found that I had to move the front seat back a little. Finding the lever on the left-hand side, like Dad always did after Mom had driven, I slid the seat back one notch. I finished adjusting the rear-view, then rolled down the window and adjusted the side mirror.

Perfect.

Having adjusted the seat and mirrors, I made sure nothing was behind the car, then proceeded to switch off the brake. I pushed the *reverse* button and, with my foot lightly resting on the brake, I slowly backed out of the garage.

I was driving! Albeit backwards, but I was driving nonetheless.

The moment I pulled out of the garage, my brother and his friend ran over to the car. They demanded to know where I was going, and shouted to whomever could hear (which was luckily no one but us) that I was in catastrophic breach of the law.

I assured them I was going nowhere. There was no need to worry and they certainly didn't have to tell on me. My brother looked at me with a smile. Give him credit—he always could sense an opportunity. "OK, but you'll owe me big time."

I made it clear that I understood. They went back to playing catch.

I was able to back the car all the way to bottom of the driveway, which went from two lanes to one as it slanted down to the road, about forty yards away. Looking back up at the garage, I pushed the *drive* button. The car lurched forward. And only lightly touching the gas pedal, I started inching up the driveway. There I was, sitting in the driver's seat of the Valiant, really driving! It was heady stuff.

After I went up and down the driveway at least a dozen times, I decided I really knew what I was doing. I had taught myself, and it was a piece of cake. So the next few round trips, I went a little bit faster. Even in reverse.

I knew I should put the car back in the garage before Mom or Dad got home, but I wasn't quite done exploring. I wondered what would happen if I kept the car in neutral, revved the engine, and with my foot still on the gas pedal, pushed the *drive* button. So I tried it.

And what an incredible rush it was.

When I pushed *drive*, I was pressed back into the seat. The Valiant shot up the driveway, tires squealing like a real racecar's. And again, no harm done. So I tried it a few more times. Nothing to it. After a few more runs, I noticed that when the tires squealed, I could see a cloud of blue smoke rise from the back of the car, just like on TV. On a black-and-white television, however, the smoke was always grayish white. This was a hundred times more exciting.

I decided that I would make one last run. I backed down to the bottom of the driveway. Then I pushed the *neutral* button. After checking to make sure nothing was in front of the car, I revved the engine. This time, I pushed all the way down on the gas pedal and punched the *drive* button—and was blown back into my seat by the car exploding forward. As the tires squealed ever louder, I looked in the rearview mirror and saw the largest cloud of blue smoke I had ever seen. Just as I was thinking about how cool this was—*bam*!

I was thrown into the car door when the car collided with the front right-side corner of the garage. I jammed my foot on the brake as fast and as hard as I could, but the Valiant didn't come to a complete stop until it had reached the back of the garage. Well, that is not entirely accurate: it actually went *through* the back of the garage. Half of the shelf that ran across the back wall was now lying on the hood. I wasn't hurt, just spooked. I stepped out to assess the damage.

To say things did not look good would be an incredible understatement. Jeff ran up to me to see if I was all right. After seeing that I was, he and his friend ran off into the woods. Smart kids.

The realization of what I had done began to sink in.

Yes, the front end of the car was sticking through the back of the garage. But that was just the start of my problems. Where I had hit the front corner of the garage, there was now a large cloud of flying carpenter ants soaring into the sky and all over the garage floor. And the front of the garage was leaning to the right, causing the right side of the garage to droop considerably lower than the left.

I am not sure if, at the time, I fully grasped the situation I was in or the futility of my actions in responding to it. When Mom and her friend pulled into the driveway not soon after the "event," they saw me trying to lift up the front of the garage with a long two-by-four. I'm sure they also noticed the ants and the Valiant's final resting position. As they stood next to me in disbelief, Dad pulled into the driveway. I can still recall what he said as he walked over to us. "Son of a bitch. What'd he do this time?" By the time he reached my mom and her friend, the answer was obvious.

I nearly went into shock when, instead of removing me from this plane of existence, my dad calmly said, "Maggie." (He called my mom Maggie most of the time, although her name was Nancy. I have no idea why.) "It looks like Ricky has uncovered a serious carpenter ant problem. We'll need to get that taken care of right away." Then he walked into the house, muttering to himself along the way. Mom's friend, taking skillful advantage of the moment, simply left.

Mom faced me, putting one hand on my shoulder and the other hand palm up. "Place them in my hand. Now."

I dropped the key fob as requested. Then Mom directed me to the back of the garage, where we surveyed the damage. What was remarkable was that, except for a very small dent in the right hood, there was no real damage to the Valiant. The garage, on the other hand, would need a good deal of work.

THE CARDINAL

Nestled next to our house, alongside a row of tall, thick pines, was an old flowering dogwood tree. It stood at least twenty-five feet high and was almost as wide as it was tall. In the spring it boasted beautiful white blossoms, and it was always covered in green leaves until the fall.

The tree was no more than six or seven feet from the house and the branches spread out in all directions. My parents had to frequently trim them back so they didn't touch the house. Looking out the den window, it almost seemed possible to reach out and grab a low-hanging branch.

On one of those low hangers, Dad hung a bird feeder. It was long, cylindrical, and clear, with two openings and perches on the bottom. Perhaps because the feeder was so close to the house, it sat unused by the local birds for quite a while.

One Saturday afternoon, as I walked up to the television to turn it on (no remote control back then), my eye caught a flash of something red just outside the window. I stopped in my tracks. Through the sheer curtain, I spotted a huge, bright red cardinal perched on the feeder. Before long, he saw me and flew off into the protection of the pines.

I shrugged it off and proceeded to turn on the TV. I was pleased to see John Wayne staring back at me, in action with the Flying Tigers. He was nearly single handedly defeating the Japanese Air Force. As I watched the aerial action unfold, I occasionally kept an eye on the feeder. And sure enough, after a brief period of time, that bird was back on the perch. He would eat awhile, take off, then return a few minutes later. This went on for the duration of the film.

At dinner, I told Mom and Dad about the cardinal and they were quite pleased. Of course, they admonished me not to scare the bird, and not to get too close to the window when he was there. I had no protest other than the fact they were preaching to the choir.

From that day forward, when I headed to the den to watch television, I'd usually see the cardinal on the feeder. As I entered the room, he would invariably fly away. I did notice, however, that he would return to the feeder with less and less delay as time went on.

I'm not sure how many days went by like this,

but I soon realized that when I entered the room, the cardinal no longer flew away. He would stay, look at me, crook his head back and forth, then return to feeding. He seemed to particularly enjoy the sunflower seeds as he picked them up and beat them against the perch until he had opened them.

After another three weeks or so had gone by, I looked outside and saw not one, but two birds on the feeder. There was the familiar bright red cardinal, of course. But now he was joined by a soft reddish brown partner with the same features, only smaller. I realized it must be the female. When she saw me, she immediately flew away, and didn't return for several minutes. But the male never left.

After a couple of weeks like this, the female stopped flying away when I'd move in the den. Like the male, she just kept on feeding. Eventually, I could stand right by the window and neither would fly away. They would just pick seeds from their perches and occasionally shoot me a glance. Sometimes, if I was at the window before they arrived, I would watch them fly to the feeder. They no longer had any anxiety about me being there.

My dad loved to watch the cardinals, too. I would often see him standing by the window observing them. As he did, he would read from the several books on birds that were open around him. He'd tell me what they ate, what seeds they preferred, how they lived, how they mated and built nests. Frankly, I learned more about cardinals than I ever cared to know.

Dad always made sure to refill the bird feeder well before it was empty. I sometimes offered to help him, but he said he really enjoyed doing it himself. He explained that we didn't need to unnecessarily bother the birds with too many people going near the tree, and that their nest must be close to the feeder, in the pines. That was OK with me. I had enough to do around the house. And honestly, it was nice seeing Dad interested in more than just doing chores or reading the Sunday *Times* on the weekends.

As time passed, and spring gave way to summer, our two cardinals now had offspring to feed. They were mostly young males, nearly as bright red as their father if only a fraction of his size. As they busied themselves at the feeder, none became upset or nervous when we'd watch them from the den. This went on all summer and fall and even into the winter. We learned from Dad's bird books that all cardinals, not just ours, stayed around during winter. Maybe that's why so many Christmas cards have pictures of cardinals on them.

Although Dad made sure to keep the feeder well stocked, he was thwarted one day by a serious snowstorm. We were unable to get outside, let alone around to that side of the house, and the feeder was completely empty.

After helping Dad shovel a path to the garage and through the driveway, I decided to unwind with some TV. As I sat there, I began to hear an incessant *tapping.* At first, I thought it was my brother. But then I remembered he was helping Mom set the table in the dining room. Dad had gone upstairs to change, and our dog was lying by my feet. What was this sound?

Listening more carefully, I realized it was coming from the window. I got up and walked over toward it, unsure of what to expect. As I did, I saw the male cardinal almost hovering outside—and tapping his beak on the window!

Tap, tap. Tap, tap, tap. Tap, tap.

I couldn't believe it.

After pounding out a few more *taps*, he flew back to the feeder. He looked at it, then back at the window, which meant he was really looking at me. It was like he was saying: "Hey you! Yeah, you. This thing is empty. Fill it."

I stared at him, dumbfounded, for I don't know how long. Before I knew it, he was right back at the window, tapping away. He flew back to the feeder and repeated the process several more times. I realized that we had better fill up that feeder. So I ran upstairs and told Dad about the whole amazing scene.

It was obvious from his demeanor that Dad thought I was just imagining things. The cardinal, as cardinals often do, was merely attacking his reflection in the window. As we headed back downstairs, I asked him, cleverly I thought, why we hadn't ever seen or heard him do it before. Dad had no answer; he just walked deliberately to the den. As soon as he got to the window, the cardinal repeated his performance. I was vindicated.

Dad quickly considered the spectacle, then informed me that, yes, the bird feeder indeed needed to be refilled. He said he'd be right back. When he got to the feeder, the cardinal flew to the branch above him, just a few feet from his head. The bird and I watched him carefully fill up the receptacle. Nary a seed was spilled. After setting the feeder back on the branch, Dad turned and began his trudge back through the snow. He had taken no more than two steps when the cardinal was back on the feeder picking and pecking at the seeds.

Probably to test my theory, Dad let the feeder go empty several more times during the winter. And sure enough, every time it was empty, the cardinal repeated his tapping ritual. At no other time did he do it. And none of the other birds ever did, either.

I don't know if something happened to our cardinal, or if perhaps he found a better place to live. But at some point, the whole family stopped coming. We never saw them again after that winter.

Once we realized that our birds weren't coming back, Dad stopped filling the feeder. He no longer seemed to care about cardinals. Perhaps because he felt slighted, he simply focused his attention else-where. For the longest time, the feeder just hung there empty—until one day, Mom finally took it down.

20

SAVING A QUARTER

On a good day it would take Dad almost two hours to get to his practice in New York City. He would get up very early in the morning and drive to the train station in Suffern, New York, to catch the six a.m. train to Hoboken, New Jersey. Then, depending on the weather, he'd either take the ferry across the Hudson River or the "Tubes" train underneath it to lower Manhattan, where he'd walk to his office on lower Broadway. This lengthy process would play out in reverse after work. Mom told us that he put up with the arduous commute so that, unlike him, we would know what it was like to grow up in the country.

Dad usually arrived home around six thirty on

weekdays. He'd freshen up and remove his tie and jacket before arriving at the table, where dinner was always served at six forty-five sharp. As you've probably gleaned by now, it was important to my parents that we eat together as a family.

One evening, as Dad was passing the salad bowl to my brother, he looked at Mom and stated, with no small measure of derision: "Those in charge of the train station have decided that we now need to pay for the privilege of parking there. I've been parking at that station for over ten years and I'll be damned if I'm going to give them a nickel—let alone a quarter."

He went on to explain that, from that day forward, he would just have to park in the Ramapo little league fields and trudge up "the damn hill" to the station. Apparently, parking in the fields was free.

Mom merely replied, "Yes, dear," and asked me to pass her the bowl of rice. Jeff and I said nothing, as it was obvious Dad wasn't in a very good mood.

A little later, when we were almost done eating, Dad piped up again. "Maggie, I know it's only a quarter. But there's a principle involved here. They never raised the issue in a public forum. They simply announced that from now on we had to pay to park. And that's just not right, regardless of how little they charge."

Jeff and I watched Mom smile and again say, "Yes, dear." I wasn't sure why, but somehow I knew we'd be hearing more about this. I just didn't know it would be so soon.

A little over a week had gone by since my dad's declaration of parking independence, and it had been filled with rain. One morning, Mom asked Dad to at least consider suspending his protest while the rain fell. But he was adamant. As he put on his raincoat to leave, he stated, "That is just not going to happen."

It continued to rain that whole day, sometimes coming down in buckets. At school, we heard that some of the streams and rivers were already over-flowing their banks. When the after-school sports bus let my brother and me off, we ran home but were completely soaked by the time we made it to the back door. Mom met us there and handed us each a towel. She told us to dry off, clean up, and get ready for dinner. Dad would be home shortly.

Mom laid the food on the table at a quarter to seven, but Dad had yet to show. A little later, she put the food in the oven to keep it warm. She told us to go start our homework and wait for Dad to arrive.

Not long after that, a taxi pulled into the driveway. From my room, I saw Dad get out and pay the driver before running to the back door. I got to the kitchen right as he entered, shaking the rain from his head and clothes. When Mom asked him what had happened, Dad said he was going upstairs to change and would be back down in a moment. Mom asked Jeff and me to help get the food back on the table and then to go sit down.

When Dad came back downstairs, dinner began as it usually did. As I handed him the plate of fried chicken, Mom asked him again why he was late. Without looking up, he piled chicken on his plate and informed us that the Ramapo River had flooded its banks.

No one said a word. I handed Dad the mashed potatoes, and he proceeded to inform us that the entire area around the little league fields was now submerged under four feet of water. Taking the salad bowl from Jeff, Dad said to no one in partic- ular, "There is no need to ask. You know I parked down the hill. And, yes. My car is one of many now under water."

Jeff and I knew better than to say anything. We dared not even make eye contact with one another. Calmly, while loading up her own plate, my mother asked: "Do they have any idea when you might be able to get your car back?"

"No. And I'm going to have to ask that you drive me to the station tomorrow morning, then pick me up in the evening. If that's all right with you?"

Mom smiled. "Of course, dear."

For the rest of dinner, nothing more was said about the car. Dad said little to nothing at all. Mom asked us how our day went, and we mumbled our quick summaries, but other than that we ate in silence. After dinner, we cleaned up our plates and went to our rooms.

The next morning, we woke up to find that, although it had stopped raining, ice now covered everything. The bushes, trees, driveway, and even the grass were now encased in a thin icy glaze. It was quite a sight.

I volunteered to go with my parents as Mom dropped Dad at the train station. On the way, Dad apologized for imposing the inconvenience, though Mom would have none of it, shaking him off as he spoke. "Mort, it's no problem at all. If you remember, I did this when the boys were just babies. It was no bother then, and it's certainly no bother now."

As we neared the train station, we passed under the bridge that held the tracks leading in and out of the station. Emerging from the other side, we could see the station and its now-paid parking lot on our left, while on the right was the rather steep hill down to the three little league fields. Dad said, "Maggie, head down to the fields. I want to see how the car fared last night."

We made it about halfway before Mom stopped the car. What we saw in front of us was tops. And I mean that quite literally. Just the very tops of the dugouts and the backstops, and the rooftops of the cars. Everything below was not only underwater, but also covered with a layer of ice.

Dad surveyed the scene, a study in stoicism. "Just drop me off at the station. I'll be back tonight at the regular time unless I call you."

Several days went by before Dad brought up the subject of his car, and Mom had warned us not to bring it up. At the dinner table, he informed us that the floodwater had receded. His car would be towed to the service station at the corner of College Road and Route 59. They would spend a couple of days cleaning it up and ensuring it was in running order.

On the following Saturday morning, one of the mechanics drove Dad's car to the house. He was impressed that Dad still owned a green 1953 Oldsmobile 88 sedan. It may have been over ten years old, but it was built like a tank. He told Dad that they had dried it out, and there were no issues with mold or water damage. The engine was running smoothly and even the brakes were fine.

Dad thanked him and offered to give him a ride back to the station. The mechanic declined, saying that he would enjoy the walk. Dad checked the car over, even kicking the tires, before moving it into the garage.

A short time later, we were sitting around the table having lunch. Dad said that the $150 to get the car towed, cleaned up, and working was well worth it. Jeff commented that he never saw it look so clean or smell that good on the inside. Mom said nothing. She just asked if anyone wanted more tuna salad.

At around three, Dad announced that he wanted to run to the hardware store for a new shovel. He'd only be gone about a half hour. The rest of us were in the kitchen when he left the house.

A few minutes later, we heard him trying to start the Oldsmobile. It kept making a sound like it wouldn't turn over. I'm not sure why, but we all decided at the same time to go outside and see what the problem was. Just as we got there, we heard the ignition catch. The engine coughed, popped and sputtered. With a loud *bang*, it finally appeared to start up . . . and then we heard a *roar*, and smoke began billowing out of the garage.

We ran around the corner of the garage and saw Dad trying to push the car outside. Flames licked up around the hood and black smoke poured out of it. My brother and I ran over to help him push. We got the car away from the garage, and just before it began to slide down the driveway, Mom got the brake on. She yelled at all of us to move away. We stood there and watched the Oldsmobile burn.

When the firefighters arrived, they hosed down the garage, the side of the house, and some of the trees, just as a precaution. All the while, the car burned in the driveway.

When the fire finally died out, there wasn't much left of the Oldsmobile. It was now just a burnt out frame and engine block. Even the tires had melted. The firefighters let Dad know how lucky he was that he wasn't hurt. They also let him know that if he hadn't gotten the car outside, he likely would've lost the garage, the Valiant, and maybe the house.

A little later, we overheard Dad telling Mom that he'd have what was left of the car towed away in the morning. That he'd call their insurance agent to discuss what coverage, if any, they had for such a scenario. And that, next weekend, they would go looking for a replacement vehicle. Mom told him that all sounded good, and that perhaps he should plan on using the Valiant for a while. She also said she had some ideas for a new car, and that Pontiac had some really nice ones.

As they headed upstairs, Mom said that, besides using the Valiant to get to the train station, Dad should see if he could work out some monthly parking rates for the adjoining lot. As they got to the top of the stairs we heard him reply, "Yes, dear."

21

GO LONG

"Ah, come on, Dad! I was wide open! He was nowhere near me—an easy touchdown!"

I walked over to the fence in exasperation, picking up the ball. Then I tossed it to my dad, who seemed unfazed by my little diatribe. I added: "I juked him out of his shoes. Should've been an easy score."

He smiled, then turned to my little brother. "OK, Jeff. It's your ball, first and ten."

It was a typical Sunday morning. When we weren't raking leaves or setting inadvertent forest fires, we'd be out here in the side yard tossing the football, at least before the Giants game came on. But the Mondscheins couldn't just play a game of catch. Oh, no. At our house, nearly everything became a no-holds-barred competition.

It was always Jeff against me, with Dad as the quarterback for both of us. Dad didn't play football in school, but he was athletic. He often played tennis with an old friend, though I didn't play with him until well after I was married. I also learned from Mom that he had played basketball for Brooklyn College.

The game rules were simple. Each brother had three downs to try to score a touchdown. The end zone went from the last forsythia bush that ran along the driveway to the split-rail fence by the road, which served as the backline of the end zone (it was quite unforgiving). The line of scrimmage began at the shed, about forty yards back, and our field of play was about thirty yards wide, marked by the woods on the left and the driveway on the right.

Even though we were supposed to be playing "touch" football, things always became rather physical, so my brother and I wore helmets. Jeff had hand-painted *NY* lettering on his, which matched his Giants jersey. He and Dad were big Giants fans.

When I was younger, I had a *G* painted on my helmet, in honor of the Green Bay Packers. I had liked the Packers because they were tough. After all, they had Jimmy Taylor as a running back. He'd go out of his way to run over a guy on the other team.

But in 1961, the Minnesota Vikings were born. And after seeing the movie *The Vikings,* with Tony Curtis and Burt Lancaster, my fate was sealed. You see, the Vikings were fearless. They pillaged and plundered wherever they went (at least in the film). Even the football Vikings played in the snow—without heaters on their side of the field. They may not have won many games in the beginning, but they looked tough, and I liked the team's colors of purple, yellow, and white. So I had my new team. And I had my Viking horns painted on the sides of my helmet to go with my Vikings jersey.

At the start of each game, we'd flip a coin to see who went first on offense. Dad may have been the quarterback, but Jeff and I would call the plays. And they were always pass plays. Regardless of how far we could get down the field, the rule was that we had to score, or it was as if the pass was incomplete. More often than not, we'd call for the long ball, figuring it was our best chance for a touchdown.

It was always fun, but the competition was real. Apparently, Dad enjoyed pitting us against each other. I'm still not sure if he aimed to use the competition to make us better, or for some other reason. But just a few downs into each game, the desire to win overtook the urge to just have fun. Shoving and tackling replaced the supposed two-hand touch our rules called for.

There was another issue that colored those games. I was (and am still) convinced that Dad wanted Jeff to win. How can I make such a claim? In my dad's own terms, the evidence on the field left no reasonable doubt. In the game's key moments, after I had run a route that Frank Gifford would've applauded, or feinted and juked my way open like Paul Flatley,

Dad would almost invariably miss the mark.

On the flipside, I often marveled at just how precise a passer he could be when tossing a perfect spiral to Jeff in a critical game situation. He'd fire it into the only possible spot where I'd be unable to intercept the ball or knock it down.

The games were always close. There were no blowouts. But when the game was on the line, the ending became predictable. We all knew who would get the misfired pass, and who would get the Hall of Fame throw into the corner of the end zone for the winning score. It got to the point where even my mom, who would sometimes come to watch, would shake her head and walk angrily back into the house.

I vividly recall overhearing them talking about it one night. Mom fumed. "Mort, you can't do this! Your playing favorites is going to cause real problems for both of them. It will not only affect your relationship, but theirs as well."

Dad didn't deny having fixed the outcome. Instead, he explained: "No—it will make Rick tougher. He has to learn that life isn't always fair, just like I had to learn with how my father treated my brother and me."

I'm not sure I learned the lesson that my dad had intended. I do know that it created a wall between us. A wall that I wasn't able to scale until I was much older, and a father myself. It did, however, make me more sensitive to treating others and especially my own children fairly.

After hearing that conversation between my parents, it also became easier to understand why I was a Vikings fan while my dad and brother were Giants fans. Or why I was a Red Sox booster while they cheered on the Yankees. Maybe it also explains why I chose to play ice hockey and lacrosse, two sports Jeff and Dad neither played nor understood.

For both Jeff and me, this dynamic would eventually play out in a number of ways, well beyond the world of sports. And to Dad's credit, our sibling rivalry was often constructive. It probably drove both of us to achieve things we wouldn't have otherwise.

But it wasn't foolproof. Because sometimes, I simply refused to compete. Academics are the best example.

You see, Dad graduated salutatorian of his class from St. John's Law School—and Jeff was salutatorian of his high school class. Let's just say that I graduated and leave it at that. Jeff also got a perfect eight hundred on both his math and verbal SATs. If you added both of my scores together, I barely broke eight hundred.

Then again, to be fair, I didn't even read the test questions. But I did make some neat patterns as I filled in the answer circles.

THE MIST

One weekend morning, while my parents were entertaining friends and my brother was at a sleepover, I excused myself and headed outdoors with my trusty Benjamin bolt action .22 and a pocket full of ammo.

Being fourteen, I understood that a rifle was no toy. If not handled correctly, it could cause serious harm or injury. I had taken all the safety courses. And I was, in fact, a crack shot, having won several shooting competitions at summer camp.

But when I was alone outdoors, with the Benjamin in the crook of my arm, all that knowledge didn't mean that my imagination didn't wander. That I couldn't see myself in some far off place where wild animals roamed. That I didn't sense dangers (i.e. potential targets) lurking behind every large rock, every tree, even the corner of my house. So I set off in search of what might lie in wait.

Just beyond our yard, the trees quickly became dense forest on three sides. Not a single neighbor's house could be seen from them, not even from the edges of our property. The only encroachment of civilization was the New York State Thruway, which ran along the edge of our property to the south, hundreds of feet below the cliff's edge. Although you couldn't see it from our home, the sound of trucks shifting gears late at night reminded us it was there.

The thick woods beyond our backyard eventually ended at a huge apple orchard, which went on as far as the eye could see. Granted, you could not see that far, as the land was hilly and full of trees.

To a rifleman, the deep woods always called. I was no big game hunter, but I could hold my own. And there was always something, somewhere that presented itself as a challenge to be dispatched. Now, mind you, I'm not talking about living things. (That didn't come until later.) There were no birds, squirrels, or rabbits harmed in any way during the making of this story—nor were any put between my crosshairs. Anyone who shoots will tell you that you never aim at something you don't plan to shoot.

I can still remember that day clearly. There wasn't a cloud in the sky, which was a deep, almost endless blue. The trees were full of colors—yellows, oranges, and reds from the oaks and maples to go with the greens of the pines and birches. The air was crisp. I could even see my breath.

I stalked the yard in search of danger. And find it, I did.

The dead limb hanging from the oak in the corner of the yard: *boom!*

A knot in the last post of the split-rail fence: *bam!*

The old bucket next to the garage that tried in vain to sneak up on me: *bang!*

The empty birdhouse hiding out on the edge of the forest: *see ya!*

There wasn't much that missed my hunter's eye. After spending what seemed like days in such forbidden and dangerous surroundings, I thought I'd take a breather, and go down to the end of the drive to check the mailbox. Empty.

After closing the mailbox and turning around to look up the driveway, I saw it. It was in the garage, on a high shelf on the back wall. Isolated. I could feel it taunting me, daring me, letting me know that it was safe. That I could never hit it from such a distance.

Now, there might have been something to that notion. It was a good fifty yards from where I was standing. But I was more than willing to meet the challenge. I carefully chambered a round and closed the bolt. Brought the iron sights up. And with the defiant one in the middle of my crosshairs, I slowly released my breath and squeezed the trigger.

Boom—got it! A wave of well-earned pride surged through me. Seeing my quarry dispatched with a shot worthy of even the best marksman was an event worth sharing with my friends. Heck, even my parents should know! That is, until I looked again at the vanquished target. A target that in its death throes was emitting, like an octopus, a fine black mist.

I watched in horror as the tarry mist began to fill the garage. Eventually it became an impenetrable thick fog, blocking out everything. I headed for it, increasing my speed with each step. As I neared the garage, I saw that damn fog for what it really was: a can of black enamel spray paint.

I looked at the can and then at the car. Yes, the car. My parents' brand new, white, two-door 1964 Pontiac Catalina. Well, that is not exactly accurate. It was no longer white. Every inch of it, including the windows, was now speckled with the black paint.

There was nothing to say. And there was no escaping the fact that life, as I knew it, had come to an end. I just hoped it would be swift and painless.

It is remarkable how mothers just seem to know when something is wrong. I think they have some kind of sixth sense. I know my dad didn't have that ability, but my mom sure did. And right on cue, there she was.

She looked at me. She looked at the car. She looked at the gun. She looked at that damn paint can. And without saying a word, she turned around and walked back to the house.

When she returned, Dad was with her. I hadn't moved a muscle or an inch since she left. I can't really tell you how long she had been gone, for time and place no longer mattered. They both looked at the car. Dad withheld comment before turning back to the house. That's how I knew he was really upset, because while the little things always set him off, the big things turned him stone-cold silent.

Mom handed me an old toothbrush. With no emotion in her voice, she said, "Do not come inside until you're finished." Then she left me there. There was no shouting. No words of incrimination. And there was no visible disappointment. Just the sentence, which seemed fair.

Standing there alone, with the Benjamin in my left hand and the toothbrush in my right, there are simply no words to adequately describe how alone, how small, how unworthy, and how miserable I felt.

As the sun was setting, Mom came back outside. I had worked feverishly to erase the evidence of what my hands had wrought. But alas, it was to no avail, as not one spot had been removed in my entire day's labor. Mom put her arm around me and said it was time to come in and get cleaned up for dinner.

I began to tell her how truly sorry I was. She held up her hand and said: "Don't! We know. We'll get the car painted next week." She hugged me. "You've had a really bad day. Let's go inside and have dinner. We'll figure out just what your payment plan will be for that new paint job."

23

To Halve and Halve Not

The spread laid out on the breakfast room table looked the same on almost any given Saturday morning. A platter of sliced red ripe tomatoes and Bermuda onions. A brick of butter and Philadelphia brand cream cheese (nothing whipped on our table). A wicker basket overflowing with New York bagels of every kind—plain, sesame, poppy, egg, pumpernickel, rye, salt, onion, and the infamous "everything" bagel. And, of course, cinnamon raisin bagels. They were always in a smaller basket within easy reach of Mom.

In the center of the table was the main event for Saturday breakfasts: lox. It resided on its own platter. This was not your everyday lox, either; it was Nova Scotia (or "Nova") lox. For the uninitiated, lox is cured salmon. Because Nova lox is cured in milder brine and lightly cold smoked, it tastes much less salty than regular lox. It is smooth and pink, almost like raw fish.

To many, it's an acquired taste. At our home it was most certainly acquired. If the bagels were fresh and warm (and thus did not need toasting), we would immediately slather on the cream cheese. Then we'd add a slice each of onion and tomato. Next, we layered the bagel with lox, folding thin slices over the onion and tomato until they were covered. Usually three pieces would do the trick. And finally, to make sure nothing oozed out, we placed another piece of onion on top before closing the bagel and squeezing it firmly together.

Next to each plate would be a tall glass of orange juice. It was the perfect flavor complement to the main course.

There was one wrinkle to our Saturday morning tradition: Mom had a firm "no lox" policy. She made it clear that she would never even attempt to develop a taste for it. Her MO was cinnamon raisin bagels with butter or cream cheese.

Jeff and I always looked forward to having company stay over Friday nights because they would be confronted with lox come Saturday morning. We used to get such a kick out of seeing their faces as Dad would explain what it was, or better yet, watching their expressions as they tasted it for the very first time. Like I said, it's an acquired taste.

But no matter how much lox and how many bagels were on the table, we would always finish them. There might be some cream cheese left over for another day, or maybe some of Mom's cinnamon raisin bagels (which, to put it mildly, did not play nice with lox). But the rest of the spread was devoured without fail.

Despite the favorable conditions at these Saturday morning feasts, they were not without conflict. You see, Jeff and I were not only competitive in sports and games. We also had to make sure that the other did not get more of anything, ever, regardless of what "more" was. We were hell-bent on being treated the same and getting the same. Immature, perhaps, but that's the way it was.

And so, if Jeff had two bagels, I would have two bagels. If I had two glasses of orange juice, he had to have two glasses. That was easy enough to manage. But it did not stop there.

Jeff and I would carefully watch each other make our bagel sandwiches. If I put four pieces of lox on my bagel, he did the same. If he added two tomato slices, so did I. This might not seem like a very big deal. But as the meal progressed, and the lox supplies diminished, things became quite serious. After all, fairness and justice were at stake.

Dad paid no attention to our sparring. He simply enjoyed his meal, eating what he wanted: usually two fully stuffed bagels. After eating he'd sip his coffee and chat with Mom about the chores that needed to be done that day.

While holding her household strategy discussion with Dad, Mom would watch us like a hawk. And, sure enough, when we got to that last piece of lox or bagel, she would step in. She'd remind us that we both already had plenty to eat, and that we could certainly figure out how to divide up what was left. And yet, Jeff and I would share a smirk, then make a grab for the goods. The triumphant one would declare, "I got the last piece. It's mine."

Without missing a beat, Mom would ask us both: "Must we go through this every Saturday morning?"

Jeff and I quickly voiced the obvious answer: "Yes."

She'd shake her head, and with just a hint of annoyance, declare, "Fine. This morning, Jeff."

OK, to be fair, sometimes she called my name. But the truth is, it didn't much matter. You see, having your name called only meant that you would take the last bagel (stuffed with whatever condiments were left) and cut it in half. After cutting it, the other brother got to pick the piece he wanted.

It always surprised me how carefully Jeff or I would cut that bagel. If one half was any larger than the other, it was imperceptible to the naked eye. It was amazing, really.

Mom employed the same technique when all kinds of different food items were at stake: pies, cakes, casseroles. Thanks to her, Jeff and I learned to cut two perfectly equal halves from just about anything.

24

YOU MISSED! NO, I DIDN'T!

I was beyond frustrated. I mean, my plan had worked, or so I had thought. Moments earlier I had positioned myself perfectly, completely hidden under a big pile of leaves and sticks. The brush was even spilling out of my pockets: a perfect camouflage outfit.

My brother and his two friends had walked right into my trap. I leaped up at the optimal moment and laid down a withering fusillade from my Mattel Tommy Burst Sub Machine Gun. It fired ten rounds in a single burst in multi-shot mode, and all I had to do was pull back the bolt to let loose another ten. Jeff's two friends (who had real integrity, I thought) had immediately fallen to the ground. But not Jeff. He had the unmitigated gall to yell, "You missed me, you missed me!" as he ran around the side of the garage.

I shouldn't have been, but I was shocked. Dumb-founded and enraged at the same time. I protested that I simply could not have missed him. He had been standing in between his two friends, only a few feet in front of me!

I was really getting tired of this. Jeff would never just admit that I *got him*. Miraculously, he either ducked, turned sideways, jumped, or benefited from the apparent incompetence of the shooter. This would happen every time, whether we played soldiers, cowboys and Indians, or cops and robbers. It made no difference which side he was on. Sometimes I wondered why I bothered to play with him at all.

With this terrible injustice in mind, I came up with an idea. A brilliant idea, I thought at the time. It would once and for all eliminate our little problem.

Perhaps I was ahead of my time. After all, today's paintball wars certainly remove any doubt as to whether or not someone has been hit. But we had no paintball guns at the time. What we did have was BB guns.

Being teenage boys not only meant that we were creative, but that the possibility of actually being hurt by our actions never entered into the discussion. Let alone into the thought processes that we might have (on rare occasion). As far as I was concerned, the bottom line was that when one of us got hit, everyone would know it.

I had a Pump Action Model 25 Daisy, which

resembled a shotgun. But more importantly, I owned the Lever Action Model 1894 Winchester BB Rifle. It was an exact replica of the classic rifle that won the West.

When I explained my idea, Jeff seemed reluctant. But then I asked him, what could he possibly have to lose? I was obviously a lousy shot, since I "always missed him." I think my brother realized that he had to either agree to play or admit he'd been lying all this time. I could tell by the look on his face that he didn't like his choices. Reluctantly, however, he agreed.

We decided that we wouldn't involve any friends. This standoff would concern just the two of us, *mano a mano*. We agreed that there was to be no aiming for the head or face. We would wear our football helmets and ski goggles, just in case. And despite the summer heat, we would wear sweatshirts and jeans.

Not long after laying down the ground rules, everything fell into place. Mom told us that she was heading out with Dad for an afternoon of shopping. As Dad climbed into the car, he said to have fun and to be nice to each other. We both assured him that we would.

After watching our parents pull out of the driveway, we went into the house to prepare. I handed Jeff the Model 25, which held fifty BBs, along with a box of ammo. I armed myself with the Winchester 1894, which held forty rounds, and a box of additional BBs that I knew I wouldn't need.

I put on a heavy-duty gray sweatshirt, jeans, ski

goggles, and helmet. Jeff geared up in a blue New York Giants sweatshirt and jeans, along with his head gear. Before announcing *go,* we added one final rule: no shooting in the house. Outside, however, was a free-fire zone and would remain so until someone was hit.

Jeff said that he'd hide outside. I would have to hunt him. Obviously, he felt he was taking the tactical advantage. But I was OK with it, because I had a pretty good idea of what he was planning. And if I was right, I would nail him before he even knew what hit him.

After watching the front door close behind him, I waited the agreed-upon five minutes before making my move.

Along the north side of the yard, there was a row of pine trees that I had used to build a "sniper's nest." From it, one could survey the front of the house, the front yard, and most of the driveway. I had deliberately made sure that Jeff had seen me putting the finishing touches on that perch. I knew he would try to use it against me.

The first thing I did was to open the front door, just to get his attention. I wanted him to think I was going to exit the house that way. Instead, I ran to the den, then ever so quietly opened the door and slipped outside.

I pressed myself against the side of the house. I was now hidden behind a row of small hemlocks and taller pines. This tree line ran roughly to the pines where Jeff was likely hiding. I couldn't see him through the branches, but I could imagine him clearly, sitting there, frantically scanning the grounds to get a read on me.

As I watched his assumed position, I noticed Lassie leaving the house through the front door. I knew Jeff would follow the movement of the dog, so I didn't hesitate to initiate my attack. I swiftly moved to the corner of the tree line where I thought he was perched. He might have had a panoramic view of the house and front yard, but he didn't have a view of what was behind and now below him. Me!

Had I not known about the perch, I probably wouldn't have been able to locate my brother. But there he was. He was about halfway up the middle pine, maybe twenty-five feet above the ground, sitting comfortably on the perch. I had made it by lashing two four-by-one planks to two rather thick branches, forming a flat bed on which to sit. Jeff had his rifle sitting on top of the two-by-four I had mounted as a gun rest. It was a superb sniper's nest, but unfortunately for my brother, I knew where it was vulnerable.

As I edged closer to Jeff, my major concern was not attracting the attention of Lassie. If she saw or heard me, she would naturally run over, giving away my position. So I just knelt there, motionless. I watched through the trees as she meandered around the front yard. Then, I saw her perk up her ears. I was afraid I'd been discovered. But, instead, she stared in the opposite direction. I followed her eyeline and saw a huge squirrel sitting on his haunches, staring back at her. I heard a loud huff, and Lassie began to move in its direction. Apparently there would be two battles that day.

I was confident that Jeff would be intently observing the same conflict between squirrel and dog. So I took the opportunity to close the gap between us, then knelt behind a small pine underneath him.

Now I saw him clearly. He sat cross-legged on the platform, rifle pressed against his shoulder and nestled on that gun rest. A classic shooting position. It would have been perfect, if only I hadn't been behind him, his back in the crosshairs of my trusty Winchester.

Knowing that my brother's position restricted his movement, I calmly laid down the gauntlet: "Hey, Jeff. Tell me I missed this time." And with that, he gave out a short yelp, even before I gently squeezed (not pulled) the trigger.

25

THE AIR DUCT

Our home was built in the early 1930s. It was a Cape Cod-style house, and after several additions over the years it became rather large. When I reached the age of ten, I was finally allowed to move out of the bedroom across the hall from Mom and Dad, which I had shared with my younger brother. I was given the new, large room off the dining room, on the south side of the house next to the driveway. It had been added when we put in a breakfast nook.

It was a simple setup, but it was mine. Golden wall-to-wall carpeting. Bed against the west wall. Dresser under the windows on the south. A desk made from an old door, with a couple of three-draw cabinets at each end. And, on the wall next to the door, my gun rack. That's where I kept my Daisy and Winchester BB guns, and when I was older, my Benjamin bolt action .22.

Mom said it was *my* room. And as such, I could decide how it would look. So my parents, on a weekend soon after I had moved down, painted it and put up the faux-dark-wood wallpaper I had asked for. Well, truth be told, Mom did most of the work. Dad just handed her what she asked for.

Dad was a really good attorney, once even getting a woman off for drug possession because of a two-minute-long break in the chain of custody. But he didn't have much practice in working with his hands. Mom, the former navy nurse, was our go-to person when something needed to be done or fixed around the house.

This new space was my fortress to the world (as the old room was now Jeff's). Our parents honored our privacy as long as we maintained our rooms. That meant we kept them clean, made the beds, and did not throw our stuff all over the floor. So no one entered without knocking—not even Mom and Dad.

I explored every inch of that room. I even checked the heating duct in the floor. One day, I noticed a second air duct in the opposite corner. Upon closer inspection, I found that its cover was not screwed in.

Peering in, I noticed that it had an opening about a foot wide and foot-and-a-half long. Then it dropped straight down, about two feet, before taking a ninety-degree turn to the right. In other words, here was a reachable, but oh-so-hidden, space. A secret space. My secret space.

As I got older, I would stash all my best stuff there. Stuff that a teenage boy savors: cigarettes, a can of beer, my *Playboy* collection. All now stored away from prying eyes or inquisitive younger brothers.

Until, that is, one fateful day during my sophomore year in high school. Just having gotten home from lacrosse practice, I heard my mom's voice. She called out evenly but firmly: "Rick, I need to see you. Please come to the living room."

I wracked my brain, trying to figure out what I had done—or more to the point, what she might have found out about. But it was a long list, and I knew there wasn't enough time to crack that nut. So, with trepidation, I entered the living room and sat down on the couch across from her.

I was perplexed. She didn't look angry or even disappointed. Although she wasn't exactly smiling, there was a touch of amusement in her eyes as she began to tell me about the man who had come to clean the furnace. About his suggestion that she clean out the air ducts in the house. And about how she had done just that, this afternoon after work, which had led her to the air duct in my room.

As a fifteen-year-old boy, I wanted to simply disappear, to close my eyes and pop up someplace else. But after trying, I found that I was still sitting there.

Mom continued by saying that she had dusted everything. That I would find it all exactly as I had left it (although she seemed to hedge on the "all" part just a bit). But, she said, that is not what she wanted to talk to me about.

My heart skipped a beat—maybe two. Then she put an end to the suspense, and cut to the chase: she had found my collection. Yes, *the* collection. And she wanted to let me know that she was concerned.

I wanted to slide down and under the couch. I mean, this was my mom, talking to me about my *Playboy*s.

"Rick, dear. You need to know that women don't really look like they do in those magazines. I don't want you to be confused or disappointed."

To say I was embarrassed would be a woefully inadequate description of how I felt. I just sat there, frozen to the spot, wishing that this was all a terrible dream but knowing that it was not. And then, Mom let me know that was all she had to say. She had to go fix dinner.

I don't remember walking back to my room. But I do remember checking my stash. And sure enough, it was still there. Dusted and neatly stacked. Even the cigarettes were still there, but somehow the beer was missing. I certainly was not going to ask about it. No sir, not me.

That was the last time either one of us spoke about that afternoon. At least, until I was married and attending a law conference in Las Vegas. I called Mom from there and let her know how the conference was going. I then asked if she remembered the talk we had when I was fifteen, about how women really didn't look the way they did in my *Playboy*s. She laughed and said that yes, she certainly did remember it.

"Well, Mom, they do exist. And they live in Vegas."

26

TARGET ACQUISITION

When I was young, I built a lot of plastic models. There were army tanks, racecars, muscle cars, ships, and airplanes. I preferred making the planes of World War II. Jets weren't really my thing.

I would spend hours building each one and painting them as they really appeared, decked out with the appropriate markings and always in 1:72 scale. This way, you could tell just how each plane compared to the others. My favorite was the P-38 Lightning, although I also built Flying Tiger P-40s, Corsairs, F6F Hellcats, the Navy's Douglas DBS Dauntless, and the British Spitfire. Of course, there were also the bombers: B-17s, B-24s, B-25s, B-26s, and B-29s. I also built the PB2Ys, known as the Flying

Boats, and the British de Havilland DH.98 Mosquito.

I did not, however, build the planes of the Japanese or the Germans. No, there would be no enemy planes in my room. My ceiling was strictly an Allied Zone. Each plane's distinctive markings declared to any onlooker or would-be enemy its squadron and nation of origin, be it the U.S. or the U.K.

The planes were arranged precisely, either in formation or attack mode. Some dove, others climbed, and some took impossibly tight turns. At any one time there must have been fifteen planes hanging from my ceiling.

I spent a lot of time just looking up, imagining what it was like to fly those fighter planes or bombers. To be engaged in dogfights. To listen to the chatter on the radio. To experience the fear and tension in the air, as each pilot battled to protect his wingman and to stay alive.

As they say, for everything there is a season, and I found at a certain age that the model planes were now just that—plastic models. It was time to move on to other things. And what better way to make room for other things than to use my models as targets for my 1894 Winchester Lever Action BB gun?

Sure, I had paper targets that I had been firing at every day. But the model planes would provide me with an opportunity to do more than just shoot. I could become actively engaged with them. No more wondering what it must have been like—now I could actually shoot them down. Of course, I would have to pretend that they were taken over by enemy pilots, and that only I could stop their secret mission.

Yes, sir. I liked this idea a lot.

It was a Saturday morning and Mom and Dad had taken my brother to his Little League baseball game. I got the step stool from the kitchen and carefully took down the US Navy dive bomber and the British Mosquito from the ceiling.

I carried them outside. And crossing the back yard to the beginning of the woods, I found just what I was looking for. I placed the planes on the ground, then went to the garage and dug a spool of fishing line out of my tackle box.

When I got back to the planes, I tied one end of the line to a tree branch, as high above my head as I could reach. Then I spooled out about twenty feet and ran the line across to another tree to the left. Pulling it taut, I tied off the line at a height just above my waist. This created a nice downward slant from one tree to the other.

Next, I tied a paperclip to a dive bomber and hooked the paper clip around the high end of the fishing line. When I let go, the plane flew along the fishing line the entire distance to the next tree. It came to a stop where the line was tied off on the other branch, swinging back and forth.

Perfect.

It didn't take long for me to bring the rest of my models out to the tree, or to load up my Winchester. On my last trip outside, I told Lassie that she had to go in the house, as I didn't want her to get hurt in the course of my mission. It was obvious she wasn't happy, but she was a good dog and did as she was told. I shut the door behind her.

I was set up with the house behind me. Though it may surprise you, occasionally I did learn from past transgressions, and I didn't want to deal with any black mists today. Now I just had to figure out how to release the planes so that they would fly down the line while I maintained my shooting position. I wondered what I might do, and then, *voila*, I had it.

I raced around the garage, found the clothesline, and removed one of the clothespins. I then cut off another thirty feet of fishing line and tied one end to the top of the clothespin. I re-hooked the paper clip to the dive bomber and to the main fishing line. Then I hooked the clothespin to the line just ahead of it. It held the plane nicely in place.

So, for the engineering challenged, I now had my original setup, but with a clothesline stopper (which was tied to the new thirty-foot line in my hand) keeping the plane in place.

I walked back to where I had left my rifle, letting the thirty-foot fishing line slide through my fingers as I went. Once in position, I pulled the line and watched as my plan worked flawlessly. The clothespin popped right off the main line and the plane began to fly down as it had before. I repeated it several times. It worked perfectly each time.

Soon I had lined up all my planes on the ground,

as if they were waiting their turn to taxi down the runway. Then I chambered a round and got into shooting position. With the navy dive bomber in my sights, I pulled the second line and released the clothespin. The plane began to pick up speed as it flew down the line. I aimed and fired and watched as the tail exploded and fell away, making the plane seesaw back and forth before plummeting from the line. It had worked!

Next came the process of methodically shooting down the enemy as they mounted their dastardly attack on our base. It was like shooting fish in a barrel. Before long there were tails, fins, wings, propellers, even cockpits scattered all over the ground under the line. Eventually I was able to get off two or three shots as the planes flew by, making direct hits each time. Nothing was getting through my withering anti-aircraft fire.

I positioned the last plane—my favorite, the P-38 Lightning—on the line. I secured the clothespin and was just about to release it when I noticed movement to my left, on the tree the P-38 would be traveling to. There, on that very branch, was a sparrow. He was just perched there, looking at me. I stood absolutely still and watched him.

As I stared at the sparrow, I let the line holding the clothespin drop from my hand. I moved the Winchester to my shoulder, slowly raising the barrel until the sparrow was lined up squarely in my sights. In military terms, this process is known as target acquisition—the detection, identification, and location of a target in sufficient detail to permit the effective employment of weapons.

That is precisely what I had been doing all morning: detecting, identifying, and employing weapons to shoot down enemy planes. Now, some twenty-five or thirty feet in front of me, I had acquired another target. A moving target. And I had it in my crosshairs.

I remember, as if it were yesterday, pleading with that little sparrow to fly away. To let me finish my business with the P-38. But it did not. It remained on that branch, moving a little back and forth, but never flying away.

I really don't remember squeezing the trigger. I felt the rifle buck slightly. And I saw the sparrow jump up and then fall to the ground.

"No!"

I dropped the rifle and ran to where the bird lay. I scooped it up in my hands and watched its tiny head flop lifelessly over to one side. I noticed the small red stain on its chest. And I knew it was dead.

I had done the unthinkable. I had taken a life—an innocent life. As my tears flowed, I begged the sparrow and God to forgive me. After tenderly laying its body down on the ground, I went to the garage to get a shovel. Then I picked up the bird and carried it to the corner of the yard, where I dug a small grave. I placed the bird gently into it, then covered him up and filled in the hole while pleading again for forgiveness.

I cleaned up all the model plane pieces. Then I took down the fishing line, put my rifle back on my gun rack, and lay down on my bed. Once there, I couldn't help it: I wept like I hadn't wept in years.

Perhaps I had passed through some necessary ritual, a rite of passage on the road to becoming a man. That may have been true in another time, but it was certainly not true in that moment.

No, I had to come to terms with the knowledge that, just because I could, I had ended the life of another living, breathing being.

27

BREAKING THE BARRIER

Sundays in the fall meant professional football. But more importantly, it meant that my friends and I got together to play our own game.

The side yard, where Jeff and I played our arguably fixed games, was perfect for football. It was almost as wide as a real field and a tad over half as long, ideally sized for four or five guys per team. When we were younger, we played with bigger teams, but some of those guys had graduated to the high school team and no longer joined us.

Those of us still playing at 12 College Road were not big enough to play on the high school team. Most of us played other sports: lacrosse, ice hockey, wrestling. But we all loved to play football. It was almost always Gimp, AK, Skipper, Spider, EJ, Heavy, TO, and me. Occasionally, my brother and one of his friends would join us.

We never wore helmets or uniforms. But we did wear our favorite college or pro football sweatshirts. And we always played tackle football. Yes, tackle. No two-hand touch or flag football for us. We tried touch, but arguments always ensued as to who touched whom and who missed. It's difficult to argue that no one touched you when you are prone on the field. (Kind of like it's hard to argue you've been shot by your older brother when sporting a fresh BB wound.)

In the old days, we'd play at Bugs' house. But after one of his cousins ran head first into a tree, hurting himself badly, Bugs' mom forbid us from playing there (or with Bugs anywhere). But my side yard was much better, anyway. There were no trees in the middle of the field.

We never kept the same teams. We were always changing them, sometimes even halfway through a game. Some of us had great hands and could catch. Others had cannons for arms, or could run like tanks and just plow people over. We always tried to pick sides so that they were even. We were all competitive, but we mostly just wanted to have a good time.

We would play for hours, stopping only for snack and drink breaks. Like in my matches against Jeff, each side had three downs to score. The games were rough. We all, at one time or another, had ripped shirts, torn pants, scratches, even bloody noses. But no one got seriously hurt. Well, come to think of it . . .

One Sunday, the whole crew was assembled on the gridiron. After lunch, we planned to watch our Suffern Mounties play the Tigers of Spring Valley. They were our archrivals. No one was going to miss that game, so we kept things moving.

Mom had provided us with paper cups, a jug of lemonade, and Oreo and Fig Newton cookies. We had finished it all off and were already well into the second half, locked in a 49–49 tie. With time running out, we kicked off, having just tied the game.

The offense marched down the field on what should have been the final drive of the game. I was on the defensive line. After the snap, Heavy and I were to count to three and then rush AK, the quarterback.

On *three*, we charged. Spider was able to block Heavy, but I barely missed hitting AK's arm before he released the ball. I ran into him and we both hit the ground—rather hard, I might add. I was lying on the ground still tangled with AK when we heard a loud *snap* and blood-curdling screams.

We stood up and looked downfield. TO, Skipper, EJ, and Gimp were all rolling around on the ground. But they were no longer in my yard.

Apparently, the four of them had simultaneously gone for the ball, which had been thrown to the back of the end zone. The problem was that the end zone ended at the split-rail fence. They had all arrived at it at the same time.

The football was still rolling around in the middle

of the road. And my four friends remained on the ground beyond the back of the end zone, surrounded by fence rails that were now snapped neatly in half.

We ran over to see if they were all right, but I first noticed that the fence was not. The posts were still there, and the lower rail was unscathed. But the middle and top rails would need to be replaced. Now, that might not have been what most people would check first. But this was no ordinary split-rail fence: it was my dad's fence.

The boys were all holding their sides: two their right, and the others their left. Spider, Heavy, and EJ were trying to help them up as I held up a part of the fence. "I think we should call the game," I declared.

AK looked at me in protest. "We have one more down left."

I motioned to the broken rail and replied, "Nope, not any more."

We got the wounded to their feet. The four of them lifted up their sweatshirts and we could see that their sides were already turning black and blue. Then we heard Skipper exclaim, "Wow, would ya just look at that."

I can still see his arm. It was bent at the elbow, in the opposite way that arms are supposed to bend. I also recall him saying: "You know, it really doesn't hurt unless I try to move it."

Of course, only a few seconds later, the shock wore off. Skipper began hollering like a banshee. Tears flowed. Even though we all fancied ourselves tough, no one could blame him for crying.

The sound brought my parents outside in a hurry. And Mom, being the nurse that she was, went to work. She would call Skipper's mother and take him to the hospital. Dad, on the other hand, evaluated the condition of the fence. He told us to pick up the broken pieces and to carry them back behind the garage. He then instructed us to get two good fence rails from the far shed.

I must admit that it was no problem getting the fence to look just as it did before the end zone incident. Unfortunately, Skipper's arm could not be fixed so easily. But at least he was still allowed to play. After it healed, anyway.

Getting my parents' permission to play football in our yard again was another issue altogether.

28

CRY HAVOC

We marched in two separate, parallel groups through the woods behind my house. Gimp, EJ, and Heavy were on one side and Skipper, TO, and I were on the other. We were dressed for stealth. We might not have had real camouflage clothing, but green or brown sweatshirts and jeans worked almost as well in the woods. Each of us was armed with a BB gun and a slingshot. And each side had a bazooka.

That's right, a bazooka. We used the old gutter downspouts from the house after Dad had replaced them with new ones. They were each about six feet long. Although originally white, we painted them green for obvious reasons.

Each team carried plenty of ammunition. Not just

BBs: five skyrockets and five cherry bombs per side. We were never sure how Skipper was able to get those fireworks, but he always came up with the goods. All of us had disposable lighters to send them flying.

This was war. And you know quite well by now my childhood policy on live versus fake ammo. I imagine this was why Jeff wanted no part of playing with us.

The rain had stopped and the sun was shining. The woods were still wet, but we knew it had to be this way. Our outfits were soaked, but the last thing we wanted was to set the woods on fire. We also knew that we had to stop playing before dark. We didn't want the rockets to be seen by parents or child spies.

The woods were a mix of pines, oaks, maples, and thick brush. After maybe fifty yards, it opened on an area almost the size of a football field that consisted of briars, thickets, and small sassafras trees. We enjoyed chewing on the bark of those sassafras trees, so we made a habit of grabbing some whenever we crossed the field.

On the other side of the clearing was a dense forest of mostly thick pines and evergreens. It sloped uphill, not steeply, but the thick brush and pines made climbing a real effort. It ran maybe half a mile and ended at a huge orchard, where the rows of apple trees extended as far as the eye could see.

The perimeter of the orchard was lined with dead trees that had been cut, cleared, and piled all along it. They were quite difficult to maneuver over and through. But they also provided great fortifications.

This is where we would do battle.

It had been determined earlier that we would defend and they would attack. The other group now moved north along the perimeter and we moved south. Not long after separating, and after walking around a large fallen tree, there in front of us stood what could only be described as the perfect fort. We didn't have to do anything other than walk through the slim opening into a small, flat, clear area.

Inside, it was maybe fifteen yards wide and the same distance long. The fallen trees and roots formed solid walls around four feet high. In the east corner, closest to the orchard, the cut-down trees formed a roof. The enclosed area was about the size of a normal room. In addition to the roof, it was completely protected on three sides by felled trees. We all agreed that it was ideal.

The first order of business was to establish how best to defend our stronghold. That meant we had to figure out where to set up the bazooka, which meant determining its "field of fire." Because the three of us faithfully watched the television show *Combat*, we knew that Sgt. Saunders was always concerned with field of fire and securing a defensive position that could be held. We agreed that the bazooka should be set up facing north, with the ability to rotate west.

The overhang that formed the roof covered our east side. The south was nothing but thick briars with enormous—and, I learned, sharp—thorns. It formed a natural barrier. If someone were foolish enough to attack from that direction, we would certainly hear him coming—and we'd send in a salvo of cherry bombs to discourage any further advance.

We knew that the others, at this moment, were planning their strategy. First, they would have to locate our position. Then try to execute an attack. All of this was clear because we knew they also watched *Combat*. But the odds were heavily stacked in our favor. Not only because we were defending, which lent a natural advantage, but because Skipper was experienced with skyrockets and TO was a master with a slingshot. And I, as you well know, was quite comfortable firing my 1894 Winchester BB gun.

Another advantage: they didn't know where our fort was, or how it actually put us in more of an ambush mode than a defensive one. If we could remain hidden, they wouldn't see us until it was too late, allowing us to attack them from a secure location.

It was Skipper who first heard them approaching. Luckily, we were all sitting behind the wall when he did. We quietly took our positions. Skipper manned the rocket-loaded bazooka and I stood ready behind him with my lighter. TO was now on the other side of the opening that served as our door. He was staying low, his slingshot readied with a cherry bomb. His lighter was out so he could quickly stand, acquire his target, and fire.

We could easily hear them approaching. They were talking amongst themselves about how they were going to crush us. They were careless and loud; branch after branch snapped under their feet. Perhaps they didn't watch *Combat* as often as they had claimed. Sgt. Saunders and Lt. Hanley would never have allowed Cage, Little John, and Doc to talk while they hunted a concealed enemy.

Skipper and I had previously agreed that when it was time, I would light the fuse and tap him on the shoulder. TO knew to fire his cherry-bomb-loaded slingshot after the bazooka had done its work. So I lit the fuse and signaled Skipper, then moved to his right. I brought my rifle up to my shoulder and prepared to open up after the rocket had been launched.

I don't think I'll ever forget the *whoosh* the rocket made as it left the bazooka. Or the surprise in the other team's voices when the rocket took off in their direction, leaving a trail of white smoke before it exploded above them. Although the sound was loud, seeing all the sparks and smoke was even more impressive. Of course, before it went off, TO had unleashed the cherry bomb right on target, so that it detonated at their feet. Now that was loud—really loud. As it was going off, I was up and firing my Winchester. Raining shot after shot in their direction.

Within seconds, our foes were defeated, yelling and screaming in surrender. They threw down their weapons, rubbing themselves gingerly where the BBs had found their marks. We came out from our covered position, triumphantly cheering and slapping each other on the back. We would have given each other high fives, but those were unknown at the time. And did not appear, I've been told, until the late 1970s.

Gimp, EJ, and Heavy checked themselves over. Except for some welts and black-and-blue marks where the BBs had hit them, no one was worse for wear. We showed them our fort, and everyone agreed that we'd have to come back to use it in the future. It would be our secret place. We decided that we'd find some old apple crates to deck it out with chairs and perhaps a table.

Skipper suggested that, since we were all together, we could pretend we were under attack from an unseen, unnamed foe and use up the rest of the rockets and cherry bombs. We agreed. Gimp said he would hold the other bazooka while Heavy loaded it and lit the fuse. Skipper and I readied ours. We fired both bazookas at the same time.

We all watched as the rockets took off and sailed into the trees before exploding into clouds of sparks and smoke. EJ and TO did the same with the deafening cherry bombs. We all agreed that there was no need to shoot the BB guns. We could do that any time, any place.

After we'd fired off all the cherry bombs, we decided to do the same with the remaining rockets. As Skipper launched the last one, he aimed it straight ahead. It went off with a loud *bang* and all the sparks and smoke prevented us from seeing much of anything for a moment. But when it cleared, we saw that the rocket had snapped a small tree nearly in half. Its leaves and small branches lay on the ground around it, shredded and smoldering.

We burst out of the fort and stomped out the embers. That the woods were wet from the rain helped quite a bit. It was at this point, I believe, that TO looked at what was left of the tree and asked: "What do you think would've happened if the rocket had hit one of us?"

29

CAMPING IN THE BACKWOODS

I've always loved the adventure of camping outdoors. Whether in the Adirondack Mountains of upstate New York or in the northern New Hampshire wilderness, sleeping under the stars has always made me feel alive. Perhaps never more so than in the woods behind my house at 12 College Road.

In those days, I did not have fancy equipment. Just a sleeping bag, a two-man mountain tent, and a friend named Skipper who loved to camp as much as I did. Skipper was a different kind of guy. My dad always got a kick out of him, marveling at how such a young man could be so politically astute and articulate. He enjoyed engaging him in discussions, wherein Skipper would explain why the Republicans were good for the country and how Governor Rockefeller was improving the state. It didn't matter that, at the time, Dad was a dyed-in-the-wool Democrat. He admired Skipper's reasoning skills and his ability to carry on a conversation with an adult.

I did go camping with others on occasion, but it was usually just Skipper and me. We came to know every inch of those woods. We made our campsite in a natural, flat clearing east of our house, just a stone's throw away from a cliff overlooking the New York State Thruway. Getting there required walking to the edge of the uphill forest that ended at the apple orchard (of rocket and cherry bomb fame), then a lengthy southerly turn along the wood line. It had taken many visits and a lot of hard work, but eventually we turned that site into our own special place.

Our campsite wasn't exactly a secret, but no one, not even my brother, knew about it. Around the perimeter of the clearing, we built a four-foot-high fence. We used branches and some of my dad's lumber from the shed, lining all sides except the south, where the ravine acted as a natural barrier. We left a small opening on the northern side and installed a door there, which was really just a movable fence. At night we placed it in the opening to secure our camp.

We set up our tent on the western side of our campsite. In the middle, we dug a large fire pit and surrounded it with stones from the adjoining woods.

For a grill, we used two shelves from an old refrigerator that we'd discovered near the orchard. We connected the shelves together using copper wire from my dad's basement workshop. (I doubt he missed it.) We had mess kits, and Mom had given us some old cutlery that would work over an open fire. If our food couldn't be placed on the grates of our make-shift grill, we cooked it on a repurposed metal sheet that we'd discovered, cleaned up, and placed on the side. The whole setup was great for cooking. It was like having one of those grills you see in diners, where they prepare bacon, hash browns, and eggs to order all at the same time. Today I realize it might have given us food poisoning, but hey—it didn't.

We did not have a refrigerator. But we did have an old cooler, which we'd fill with plastic bags of ice to keep our sodas, and sometimes beers, cold. As for the latter, Skipper had, from time to time, been able to liberate some from his house. He did it in such a way that it was never missed, and we stored the spoils at the camp. There were a number of occasions during which we imbibed, but for the life of me I can't recall what we discussed or did during those times. Funny how that works.

What I do remember was the freedom we felt camping out. There was no one telling us to do this or that. Or, more importantly, not to do something.

It wasn't that we didn't work, though. We most certainly did. Camping is not easy. Skipper and I had to set up the tent and police the campsite to make sure it was clear of things that might attract wild animals. We saw raccoons, squirrels, skunks, and even deer from time to time. We never saw any bears, but we just couldn't take the chance. We also gathered and chopped firewood and kept the fire burning.

We made our own meals. Most of the time we had baked beans with chopped hot dogs, but sometimes we grilled steaks. Those are still some of the best-tasting steaks I have ever eaten. It was breakfast, though, that we both liked the best. We would bring a dozen eggs and a pound of bacon and always cook it all. We would also toast an entire loaf of Pepperidge Farm bread. There was just something special about that bread, grilled over the open fire. We never cared how toasted it got—we ate it all. And we loved cleaning up all the bacon grease with it.

Sometimes, we brought an AM transistor radio with us, and we'd listen to Cousin Brucie on 77 WABC. He was on Saturday nights until midnight, spinning great music and better antics.

One night, Skipper and I had gotten a late start. By the time we had gathered wood and made a fire, it was late and already quite dark. The fire lit up our camp, but outside the fence perimeter, it was pitch black.

We were making a large pot of Campbell's Barbecue Beans, which sadly no longer exist. (When complemented with sliced Hebrew National franks, they yielded one of the finest meals known to man.) We were listening to Brucie's show, and had just opened two cans of soda.

Suddenly, Skipper turned off the radio and asked

me if I had heard anything. I laughed, and said that I'd heard the radio until he turned it off. He shot back: "No, really. I heard something out there."

I moved over to the fence and peered through the branches. In the distance, to our north, I saw three lights that appeared to be swinging back and forth and coming closer. Now, when you're a teenage boy, the first thoughts that enter your mind in such a scenario are not pleasant. These thoughts are usually based on movies that don't end well for the campers. And we were the campers.

Skipper and I pulled our Buck hunting knives from their scabbards. No longer talking, we gave each other hand signals and moved together out of the camp, into the woods and the darkness.

Once out of the camp light, we lay flat on the ground, each with one arm in front of our faces. This was a method of concealment we learned from watching Tonto on *The Lone Ranger.* The swinging lights moved closer and closer. What was disconcerting, to say the least, was that the lights did not appear to be attached to anything. They seemed to be suspended in the air. We saw nothing around them.

When the bright lights were some forty or fifty feet from the camp, we heard what sounded like radio static. Then, a deep, low voice called out: "You, by the fire! Show yourselves. This is the police."

Skipper and I put our knives back in their scabbards and jumped to our feet. "We're over here!" The three beams of light turned immediately in our direction, lighting us up.

For a moment, neither one of us could see. Going from total darkness to police flashlights in one's eyes will do that. We heard another voice say: "Lower your lights. It's all right, they're just kids." The lights fell to our feet and our vision began to return.

The policemen walked over to the camp, checking out the fence along the way. One of them stated: "Quite a camp you've got here. You boys OK?" Skipper told them we were fine, just on a campout. I agreed, and mentioned that I lived nearby, in the house on College Road. As I spoke, one of the officers, who had not yet said anything, inspected the campsite. He stuck his head in our tent, then turned to the others and informed them that all was in order.

The officer then walked over to Skipper and me. He informed us that they had received reports about a fire in the woods, which led them here to check it out. But he quickly switched gears. He said that we had made a fine camp. He was impressed with how secure we'd made our tent, and with how well we'd built the fire pit. And with the precautions we'd obviously taken to ensure the fire wouldn't get out of hand. Another officer told us that our beans smelled delicious. Skipper offered him some, but he declined.

The officers double-checked my address, and one of them said to the others: "He lives in the house with the black-and-white collie." They told us to be sure the fire was out before we broke camp, and to be careful—but also to enjoy ourselves. And then they were off.

After the police disappeared from view, we stoked up the fire. We ate our baked beans and franks, which were delicious as always. After lapping up our dinner, we tuned back in to Cousin Brucie's top forty countdown. Then we pulled out two cold ones from the bottom of the cooler.

30

THE TENANT

It was a sunny afternoon in June. I had just gotten off the school bus and was walking home when I saw G-Man standing in my driveway. I noticed that he was wearing a backpack with a sleeping bag tied to it, looking rather forlorn. G-Man was not really a friend. A schoolmate, yes. But we were never really friendly. And he lived at least ten miles away.

I said "hi" and asked what he was doing this far from home. He told me that he had decided to run away. He just couldn't take his mom harping on him all the time, and he had gotten into some trouble at school. There was no need for me to ask what it was about. Everyone knew he was sniffing glue. And apparently, his parents had learned about it, too.

That was how he got his nickname: "G-Man" stood for Glue Man.

I asked G-Man if he had any idea where he was going to go. He looked at me with a troubled, faraway look, like he'd recently been sniffing. Without saying anything, he just shook his head from side to side.

Now, it was not that I wasn't a caring or concerned sixteen-year-old. But I knew Mom and Dad weren't going to be pleased if I had G-Man stay with me. Especially when he was almost always high. But I also couldn't just send him on his way. As we stood at the end of the driveway, I looked up toward the garage. And that's when it dawned on me: the playhouse.

The playhouse was a converted old wooden shed that was on the south side of the garage. The door faced away from the road, which meant that no one could see who was coming and going. It had been used at one time as a large chicken coop, then as a storage place for chopped wood. But now it was something just a little greater, at least as far as Jeff and I were concerned.

In the southwest corner, there was a small door that lifted straight up, probably once used by the chickens. But it was just big enough to squeeze through. The shed had two large windows facing south, covered by well-worn curtains. My parents even let us deck out the place with some old household furnishings: a throw rug, two chairs, a steamer trunk, and a single bed that we used as a couch.

This was our place. We had decorated it with

posters of our favorite cars and baseball and football players. And, of course, with a few incredible *Playboy* foldouts. It was 1966, and Melinda Windsor was Miss February, Donna Reed was Miss May, and they were both prominently displayed over our playhouse couch. Mom said she did not want to know about them.

I told G-Man to come with me. When we got to the playhouse door, I told him that he could stay there. But he had to first promise to be invisible while on the premises, and that no one could know his whereabouts. I said that I would try to sneak food to him each night after everyone went to bed.

G-Man appeared reluctant until I showed him the inside of the shed. He liked that it was clean and furnished, but I think Misses February and May clinched it for him. He looked quite pleased, agreeing it would work and that he'd hold to the pact of secrecy. I let him know that there could be no drugs and absolutely no glue on our property. He said that was fair.

Then, G-Man threw me a curve. He asked me how much it would cost him to stay.

To be honest, I hadn't even thought about charging him. But he'd asked, so I figured, why not? We agreed to fifteen dollars a week. And if I were able to get him food, we would make it an even twenty. We also agreed that if he were discovered, I would deny all previous knowledge of him being there. To seal the deal, he gave me the first week's payment in advance.

It wasn't difficult getting food to G-Man; I managed to bring him a little of everything we had for dinner most evenings. When the coast was clear at night, I'd throw some leftovers on a paper plate and wrap it in plastic wrap (usually with a soda), then quietly sneak out to the shed. Once there, I would rap three times, and then two more (our secret code). If he wasn't there, which was often, I'd simply put the plate on the trunk. I remember Mom telling Dad that I must really be working hard lately, because I was eating a lot of late night snacks.

I'm not sure what G-Man did for his personal hygiene during his stay in the Mondschein Chateau. The playhouse had no running water, no bathroom. We did have a garden hose behind the garage. But I think it's best to simply leave it a mystery.

Believe it or not, things ran smoothly through the rest of the June and for most of July. I had already made eighty dollars, and was looking forward to my next twenty, when things came to an abrupt end. Apparently life had conspired to create the perfect storm.

Mom had decided to donate another chair to the playhouse, even generously taking it there herself instead of asking me or Jeff to do it. Holding the chair in one hand, she opened the shed door with the other. I can only imagine the look on her face when she saw G-Man, standing there in front of her. Buck naked.

You might venture a guess as to what happened next, but it's doubtful you'd be on the mark. Because, remember, my mom was no ordinary mom. This former navy nurse happened to know judo. So when that door opened, it was not Mom who screamed. It was G-Man. And he didn't scream just because he was startled. He screamed because, instead of dropping the chair and running away like most people would, Mom used the chair to bring him down to the floor in one fluid move. A move that would have made Jackie Chan proud, but which left G-Man incapacitated.

Standing in the kitchen that delightful summer day, I heard my mom exclaim: "Rick! Get your butt out here—on the double, mister!" I immediately knew I was busted.

When I got to the shed, Mom was sitting on the chair, pinning G-Man down by his neck and chest. She looked at me in such a way that I can only describe as unnerving. Through gritted teeth she asked me if I knew this "gentleman."

All I could do was nod. Still on the chair, Mom let my now ex-tenant know that his stay was over. That he would be checking out. And that he was to be off the property in five minutes. As for me, I was to march myself to my room and not leave it until she came to get me or "when hell froze over," whichever came first. She then told G-Man that she was sorry to have met him this way. That perhaps in the future they would meet under different circumstances. She hoped that he would be wearing clothes at the time.

To risk stating the obvious, Mom and Dad were not pleased that I had allowed G-Man to take refuge in the shed. Nor were they delighted that I had told no one he had run away from home. So, I was grounded for a couple of weeks. And I had to wash the dishes every day for the rest of the summer.

One night, a little later that summer, I overheard my parents talking about me and G-Man again as they sat in the living room. What could I have been thinking? It wasn't all one-sided, though. At one point, I heard my mom say: "Well, he was trying to help a friend. Maybe not in the right way, but he was still looking out for him."

I dare not imagine my parents' reaction had they discovered I was charging him rent. As for G-Man, I didn't see him again until school began in the fall. We'd occasionally pass each other in the halls, but we never did speak to each other again.

31

MONDSCHEIN'S MARAUDERS

In the summer of 1967, one of Dad's clients, a Greek ship owner, invited my parents to sail on one of his vessels. The trip would span half of July and most of August, and would take them from New York City through the Panama Canal to San Francisco. Mom and Dad knew it might be a once in a lifetime opportunity, and with our encouragement, they decided to take it.

The catch was that this trip would leave Jeff and me alone (and unsupervised) for almost two months. So my parents had a close friend of the family, a sweet older woman who I'll call Tess, named as our legal guardian. Although not specifically spelled out, it was assumed that Tess would stay with us while our parents were away.

After Mom and Dad departed, I explained to Tess that there was no reason to rearrange her life just to take care of us. I was now almost seventeen, and would begin my senior year in the fall. Jeff was fifteen, entering tenth grade. We were more than able to take care of ourselves. And, I reminded her, she lived only five miles away. If we needed her, she could be there in just a few minutes. Otherwise, I would call her when my brother and I were home each night, at the specified curfew time. After some discussion (spiked with serious whining and suggestions that, hurtfully, she didn't trust us), Tess relented and agreed.

I will state, for the record, that we were always home before the established curfew of eleven. And I called every evening, right on time. However, that didn't mean that afterwards I might not slip back out.

On a Friday evening in early August, I had arranged for a number of my friends to spend the night. Probably their parents didn't realize that mine were not home. But what they didn't know didn't hurt them. So joining me (and my brother) that night were all of my closest friends: Skipper, TO, AK, Shorty, and JB. We did just about everything together in those days: going to the movies, playing sports, even double dating.

We didn't just get together this particular night in this particular way by happenstance. No, I had long been wondering about the people who lived on the other side of the road: the Schmidts. Their unpaved driveway was surrounded by large, dense pine trees as it wound back into the thick woods, disappearing around a bend to the right. The trees ran the entire length of their property along the road, so tightly packed together that you couldn't see more than a few yards in. And forget about trying to see their house.

We almost never saw the Schmidts, either. They kept to themselves. Mr. Schmidt was an older gentleman with thick, wavy white hair. I don't recall ever meeting Mrs. Schmidt, but I had seen her in their car a few times when they drove by. Dad said that they were German, and kept several German Shepherd dogs. They made him uneasy.

The few times I did see Mr. Schmidt, he was at the end of his driveway retrieving his mail. He sometimes spoke to me then, in a thick German accent. I knew it was German because I'd heard it spoken in all the war movies: *The Enemy Below, The Longest Day, The Guns of Navarone.*

Lassie had passed away that spring, but in the years prior, she would always growl and bark at Mr. Schmidt. This was something she didn't do with most people. Tammy, the puppy we got in June of that year, had yet to meet him.

So, on this night, my friends and I were determined to discover just what the Schmidts were hiding. As terrible as it might sound, we wanted to know if they were really Nazis, escaping from their past. I convinced the others that we needed to find these things out. The boys were on board: patriots, all.

We waited until after midnight to make our move. Jeff was not happy—not at all—about what we were planning. He wanted no part of it. He thought we'd get into serious trouble, and he reminded us about those German Shepherds. I told him that he didn't have to go along, but that he'd better keep quiet about it . . . or else. He promised, then stomped off to the den to watch television, muttering to himself the whole way.

Having faithfully watched the TV series *The Man From Uncle*, with Napoleon Solo and Illya Nickovitch Kuryakin, all of us knew to be dressed in dark clothing. And to be armed for the occasion. So some of us carried BB guns, others slingshots, and nearly everyone pocketknives. You just never knew what might be in those woods.

When we made our way to the end of my driveway, we had to duck for cover and lay flat on the ground as a car went by. The road was not traveled much, especially at that hour, so we should have recognized this for what it was—an omen.

I was the first to make a break for the other side of the road. When I got there, I dove into the roadside ditch. Knowing how to move quietly without being seen is not a skill one is born with. It must be learned and mastered. Thankfully, all of us watched *Combat*, so we were well aware of how to conduct a raid. And we had participated in many war games over the years.

The rest of the group followed quickly behind me. We decided to form two groups. Skipper, TO, and I would take the right side of the driveway through the woods, and Shorty, JB, and AK would take the left. We all agreed it was imperative to move with stealth and observe silence because of the dogs.

We worked our way through the woods alongside the road, which were thick with pines, small trees, brush, and thorn bushes. It was also really dark, so it was difficult to see where we were going or where we were stepping. Progress was slow. But after about fifteen minutes, we could see, flickering through the trees, the lights of a house.

Skipper, TO, and I reached the tree line, where it opened up into a clearing. There we saw the Schmidts' station wagon, parked in a circular drive that ran to the front of the house. The only light we could see was emanating from a window in the house. It filled the clearing with eerie, elongated shadows.

I was beginning to think that perhaps this was not the best idea I had ever come up with. That, just maybe, we should all turn around and go back. That's when we heard a tree branch *snap* loudly to our left. And the sound, rather than be swallowed up and muffled by the woods and darkness, seemed to reverberate off the house. We also heard a voice call out something like, "Oh, ship!" But maybe I'm a letter off. It was at that moment that the apocalypse began.

The entire yard and woods exploded into brilliant light, thrown down from massive floodlights atop tall poles. And what can only be described as an air raid siren began bellowing out an incessant wail that grew louder and louder. And then, we heard the dogs. Huge, angry dogs. With discretion, as they say, being the better part of valor, I yelled, "Run!" We all turned and sprinted back from whence we came.

Given the elements in play—the dense forest, the sirens blaring, the dogs barking, the search lights casting harsh bright lights and impossible shadows—any sense of direction was completely lost to Mondschein's Marauders. I could hear the dogs. I could hear my friends screaming. And the next thing I knew, I was tumbling over a limb and rolling through dead leaves.

As I pulled myself up, I ripped my shirt on a thorn bush. I swallowed my need to scream, opting instead to run faster, my arms doing their best to fend off the oncoming branches as they smacked me just about everywhere. And then, a new sound was added to the symphony of horrors: a loud *splash*.

Apparently, there had been a pond on the property after all. And now one of us had found it. I made it out to the road about the same time as TO. We both ran onto my property, where we hit the ground and cowered behind an oak tree. In seconds, the rest of the team emerged from the woods, joining us in our fallback position.

Skipper was the one who had found the pond: he was soaked from head to toe. I told the boys that we were not safe yet. We had to get inside the house right away. We ran around the house and entered through the back door.

In the light of the mudroom, I saw what a mess we were. Torn clothing, muddy feet, scratches all over. I told my crew to go down into the basement; I'd be back shortly. I ran to my room and stripped off my clothes, replacing them with a pair of pajamas before going to the kitchen and washing my arms and face in the sink. I grabbed a six-pack of Coke and brought it down to the guys. They were to stay there until I had fully assessed the situation.

As I came back upstairs and into the kitchen, I ran into my brother. Jeff was upset. Just like he had predicted, we were all in serious trouble now. I told him to relax, that nothing was going to happen. But I had no sooner finished saying so when we heard police sirens.

We ran to the front door and peeked outside. It wasn't just one or two police cars out there: five flew into sight, lights flashing and sirens blaring. We watched two pull into the Schmidts' driveway and disappear into the woods. Two parked on the side of the road, right in front of our house. And the last drove right up our driveway.

I raced to the basement door and told the boys to keep quiet; the police were here. And then, without even thinking, I picked up our puppy, Tammy. The sirens had gotten to her; she looked scared and bewildered. I went back to the front door with her, telling Jeff to let me do the talking. I could see that he was trying really hard to hold himself together, but he was clearly terrified.

We watched as a rather tall, big-shouldered, uniformed Ramapo police officer approached the front door. As he opened the screen, I opened the front door. There we were, standing in front of him: Jeff in his plaid pajamas and me in my blue stripes, clutching Tammy in my arms. Thank goodness I had washed my hands and face, and that the pajama top had long sleeves.

The officer looked us over. "No need to be worried, boys. We're here now." I asked him what was going on, but first, he wanted to know where our parents were. I told him they were out. I didn't think it prudent to let him know that they were at this very moment somewhere on a ship in the Panama Canal. Nor would it have been wise to explain the "arrangement" I had negotiated with Tess.

As the officer scratched Tammy's ear, he asked if we'd seen anything strange that evening. I told him we hadn't, but that we had heard a lot of dogs barking and a loud siren. He nodded, and said there'd been a problem across the street, but that everything was all right now—no need to worry. I thanked him and shut the door. Jeff and I did not take our eyes off of him until he got back to his squad car.

I told Jeff that the crisis had passed, so he should go to bed—it was close to one in the morning. I also reminded him that it was in both of our interests if he said nothing about what happened to anyone. Especially Mom and Dad. He promised while muttering something about jail, but I didn't hear all of it and didn't really care to.

I returned to the basement and filled in the gang about my encounter with the police. We realized that we'd all dodged one heck of a bullet, that life as we knew it had nearly ended that night. We laughed and hugged and slapped each other on the back, releasing all the evening's tension. It was then that TO noticed the pajamas I was wearing. And that I was holding Tammy.

I didn't even realize she was still in my arms. We patted her and scratched her tummy as the guys kidded me about how innocent I looked. Frankly, I'm convinced that when the policeman saw Tammy in my arms and my brother and me in our pajamas, there was just no way that we would have been considered *persons of interest.*

The police cars didn't leave until after two that morning. After they departed, the guys came upstairs. They washed up and changed, then we crashed on the den floor in sleeping bags. As we lay there, we took stock of the situation: we had all made it back, some more fit than others, with a few weapons lost to the woods. We all had bumps and bruises and some had scratches. No real damage had been done. We were more convinced than ever that there was something going on in the Schmidt woods, but we were also certain that we wouldn't be the ones to uncover whatever mystery lay hidden there.

32

Would You Believe?

It was the first Saturday after Labor Day and my senior year of high school had just begun. I knew Mom was preparing a special dinner for the family and I was running late.

My parents had arrived home the previous Sunday from their long cruise through the Panama Canal to San Francisco, and they were racing to make up for lost time. Mom was beginning another year at the public school and had a lot of paperwork to catch up on—stuff she usually did during the summer. And Dad had to get back up to speed with his legal practice.

This would be our first real time together since before their trip. My brother and I were back in school and had our after-school sports programs to talk about, along with a million other things. Though it was Saturday, this dinner was to be like a Sunday dinner, with a roast, a dessert, and lots of conversation.

I had come from a friend's house, where time had gone by faster than I'd realized. After quickly washing my hands and face in the kitchen sink (I heard Mom say that I should have done so in the bathroom), I entered the dining room. I found my family sitting in the same places as always: Mom closest to the kitchen, her back to me as I entered, with Jeff to her right and Dad across from her, in front of the window. Tammy was stretched out near my empty chair.

I noticed that even though I was running late, and had apologized for it when I entered the room, neither Dad nor my brother had looked up. There was not even any of the usual sarcastic banter from Jeff about my being late. As I rounded Mom's chair, what I saw made my heart leap into my throat and my mind fly into crisis mode.

Hanging on the top left post of my chair, a colonial ladder-back, was a pair of satiny red lace panties. I stopped, rooted to the floor a mere step away, staring at my certain demise. Dad picked at the salad on his plate and my brother kept his head down. I'll always remember what my mom said next. "Since I was away for so long, I thought I'd help you out and vacuum your room. As you can see, I found something under your bed that should not have been there. Care to explain?"

Many things flashed through my mind as I stood there looking at those damn red panties. None of which I could tell my mom, or even dare repeat here. But as I went to sit down I gathered my wits about me. I explained, quite convincingly I thought, that because I had access to a car, a few friends had gathered at our house when we decided to go swimming at the lake. Some of them were girls, and they had changed in my room, you see.

I sat down, relieved. That was certainly a solid, no-frills response to Mom's question. Maybe not airtight, but close. I was proud of myself.

Are you old enough to remember the television show *Get Smart*, with Don Adams? If not, Adams played Maxwell Smart, a bumbling spy who always came out on top despite his many shortcomings. One of his catchphrases was, "would you believe?" If someone doubted the veracity of a statement he'd made, he would follow it up with that catchphrase, then give a more believable answer. Well, in response to my brilliant retort to my mom's question, she responded, without missing a beat, "Would you believe?"

Silence fell upon the dining room. Time ground to a merciless halt. There was nothing I could say that would extricate me from this embarrassing and humiliating situation. I could only sit there in my chair with those panties hanging next to my head like a badge of shame. I thought it best to remove them. As I reached back, Mom said: "No, let them be. You can deal with them after dinner. They're fine right where they are."

As I sat there, I wondered if I had been set up by the owner of that particular bit of clothing. Luckily, I didn't usually date girls from my high school, but rather those from Spring Valley, so the damage could be contained. (Or so I thought.) I had decided on this particular dating policy for two reasons: to avoid the betrayals, breakups, and jealousies I had watched my close friends go through, and to stay out of the school rumor mill. And it mostly worked. That and my penchant for avoiding the spotlight often kept me out of trouble I may have deserved. But little did I know, at the time, that girls do a lot of "talking" in the locker room. And unfortunately for me, the Spring Valley girls' gym teacher happened to be a very dear, close friend of my parents. Yes—I would eventually learn that I couldn't always outrun trouble.

I sat there in pained silence for what felt like an eternity, though it was probably only a matter of seconds in real time. Dad looked at me and asked: "So, Rick, how was your day? And oh, by the way, please pass me the salad bowl."

33

THE DINING ROOM CHAIRS

The ladder-back chairs that once graced my parents' dining room table can now be found around mine. The table is not the same; that went to Jeff, and somewhere along the line he parted with it. But I got the chairs when my parents moved from 12 College Road to the San Remo building in New York City. They relocated there after Jeff and I finally left home; Mom said it would make things easier on my dad. His office was still in the city, and over the years, the commute had taken its toll.

My children grew up around those chairs, just like I had. Though they've since moved out themselves, the chairs remain. As I sit now gazing at them, I can see my whole family. Not just Mom, Dad, and

Jeff, but Lassie and Tammy, too. I also see my children, Adam and Emily, and our Golden Retriever, Goldie. Joining them are my son-in-law, Kamal, and daughter-in-law, Yaani. And the grandchildren: Annie, Nate, and Eli. They stand near the old family dictionary, with its yellowing pages, but for now their focus remains on their Golden, Sadie.

And, of course, there is my dear wife, Ginny, who I met during the first week of college and married after our sophomore year. Ever since, we've experienced life's astonishing journey together.

Except for the ladder-back chairs and a few other small pieces, no artifacts remain from the early part of my life. Even our house at 12 College Road no longer exists. It was torn down and bulldozed over. An office building now stands on the very spot where I grew up. As for the woods, they were swallowed up by huge parking lots surrounding an indoor tennis court and an ice hockey rink. And the apple orchard is now a large development of tract homes. Even the mysterious Schmidts' place is gone, replaced with a vast complex of apartments and condominiums.

What does remain are those ladder-back chairs and the memories they hold.

Of course the moments of family crisis and triumph are there. But so are the little off-handed remarks that added color and contrast and unexpected laughs. So is the rare but moving praise given by Dad. So is Mom's knowing smile as she greeted me at the door with a hot chocolate, whether I deserved it or not. So are the memories of watching my parents hug like newlyweds in the kitchen, even as the years progressed. And so are the furtive nods between my brother and me that always meant something—and still do.

These are the memories that help me confront today's ups and downs, the moments that keep my 12 College Road family with me, even as I continue on without them.

RETURN OF THE WARRIORS

My silent warriors have returned,
With their gallant cries and muted groans.
Again, they scale impregnable barriers,
With lives that were once their own.
Their flag held high
They march in step,
To fight for values
That they once kept.
Onward they come through shell and flak,
With teeth bared and bayonet fixed.
The sound of the bugle shatters the air,
As my silent warriors charge
The now fallen fortress of the living room chair.

ESM

ACKNOWLEDGMENTS

Acknowledging the assistance of others is not difficult, but making those whom you thank understand just how appreciative you are is. I will try my best.

Normally, giving thanks to family members is saved until the end. But I must start by thanking my dear wife, Ginny. She not only encouraged and pushed me, but also read and edited the drafts, making fantastic suggestions and letting me know when I really went off the rails. To be blunt, without her, this book never would have been written. I also wish to thank my son, Adam, daughter, Emily, and nephew, Jared, who each read the initial draft and gave me the encouragement and drive to persevere throughout this endeavor.

I must also thank Phyllis Edgerly Ring, my mentor and friend, whose writing workshops provided the environment and nourishment that brought this book to life, and whose guidance, counsel, and friendship

helped deliver it. To Michael Schindler, my editor—
who pushed, motivated, applauded, taught, and
made numerous improvements to the manuscript—I
offer my deep appreciation, respect, and gratitude. I
also extend my thanks to Kathleen Kalinowski and
Douglas Moore for reading this memoir and making
insightful comments for its improvement.

And a special thanks goes to Wade Fransson, who
not only made suggestions for bettering the manuscript, but whose energy, drive, and motivation made
publishing this book possible.

I also want to give a special nod to the late Wesley
College Professor William A. Hughes, who urged me
to write when I was a freshman so many years ago. I
am sure he knows that I finally took his advice.

CPSIA information can
Printed in the USA
LVOW01s2308251113

362764LV0003